D0117951

The
SECRET
of
LIFE

Elizabeth Wurtzel

The
SECRET
of
LIFE

Commonsense Advice for
Uncommon Women

(PREVIOUSLY PUBLISHED AS
Radical Sanity)

BALLANTINE BOOKS
NEW YORK

FOR MISS MABIS CHASE,

CHRISTINE FASANO, ROBERTA FELDMAN,

JODY FRIEDMAN, AND

SHARON MEERS—OF COURSE

Contents

✳

Introduction: The Secret of Life

I am not the happiest person. In fact, in the battle between joy and misery, I'd say that the latter often seems to prevail. I don't like this, and every day I refuse, for the eighty millionth time, to put up with another minute of it. But the world does what it does, and I often find it disagreeable. After all these years, I'm kind of resigned to that.

But I do have one thing on my side: I have enormous faith. And hope. I am not speaking of the kind you find in church or in the afterlife or in heaven or in the King James Bible or in the Hare Krishnas that we all encounter changing flights in the airports of the world. I am speaking of a simple faith that says that one way or another, no matter how many times I stumble and stub my big toe, somehow life is going to work itself out.

So this is a book about mistakes. In fact, this is a book *in praise of* mistakes. May you make many of them along the way. May you make them left, right, and center, and when you do, may you never claim to have profited from them. May you never ever chalk them up to lessons learned or experience gained or any of that trite, commonplace bullshit. Just enjoy your idiocy, cry about it and bask in it, and be glad you are lucky enough to have a life that has room for some stupidity and lolling about and kicking around, because, you know, that's how it goes, and that is what it means to be living.

And there are much worse things than mistakes. There are self-importance and smugness and arrogance and all the other traits that are associated with *belief*. Belief is a good thing in principle, but an annoying thing in human beings. Faith is for people who are not possessed of belief, and faith is a much better thing. To explain: People who *believe* walk around with a certainty and ease that, in my opinion (which is always correct), they ought to be taken out and shot for. They go around full of belief, they go through life just *knowing* that they will get that plum job, *knowing* that they will meet and marry that plum boy on some perfect and preordained schedule, *knowing* that they will get that apartment on the sunny side of the street—the one with the high ceilings and bay windows and a marble bathroom and elegant detailing—for half the going rate, with no problem. They *know* they are going to win the lottery, they *know* they will always have a date on Valentine's Day—and that it will surely involve long-stemmed red roses by the dozen and a fine meal of filet mignon—and they *know* that they will always most certainly be happy, even on New Year's Eve.

Yes, New Year's Eve.

Don't get me wrong: Perhaps the lives of the true believers sound rather pleasant. I mean, how nice never to be at a loss for love on February 14, year in and year out. Far be it from me to put that down. But we all know that life doesn't work that way for anybody, and the people for whom it does get their come-uppance sooner or later—in the form of drug-addicted children or obnoxious in-laws or jail time for tax evasion as a result of the assumption that they can break the law because they believe that they have God on their side. These people end up like those treacly televangelists, like Jimmy Swaggert with his mistress naked in *Hustler,* like Jim Bakker with his paramour naked in *Playboy*—not to mention that he ended up in jail, divorced, defrauded and defrocked, with ex-wife Tammy Faye somehow still able to breathe under piles of pancake makeup. Or they end up like Newt Gingrich, who was preaching moral probity in his Contract with America—all the while he had asked his first wife for a divorce while she was in a hospital dying of cancer. Never mind that one of Newt's daughters is a lesbian. Or that his scandalous behavior got him thrown out of the leadership of Congress, and then out of Congress altogether. And he was so sure he had God on his side. But probably not as sure as William Bennett, a man so certain of his righteousness, so shamelessly sanctimonious, that he actually wrote *The Book of Virtues*—not realizing how it would look when he ended up with $8.5 million in gambling debts. Which, I don't think, is very virtuous.

That is what happens to the people who are absolute believers. They are perfectly capable of ruining their own lives. They need no assistance from you.

Just be glad you're not one of them. Trust me.

And have faith. Have faith that somewhere along the way you will manage to get all the joys in life that you hope and wish and pray for, the things you ask for every time you blow out your birthday candles, the dreams you imagine every time you see a shooting star (or an airplane that you mistake for one), or even every time you sight just a lone, regular, pretty star, hanging out in the sky, all still and peaceful and bright.

I probably want more or less the same things that you do. Being human, we all kind of want the same things, to love and be loved, and all that. And in the rules I've laid out here, I believe I have found the secret of life.

The point I must make beforehand is that I myself don't always follow my own good advice. In fact, I fuck up all the time. Indeed, I fail miserably, which might be why I am often unhappy. While I of course have no trouble wearing mascara or having pets or seeing too many movies, it is not so easy to manage not to call boyfriends I miss in the middle of the night or not to wonder if I'll ever meet a guy who doesn't drive me crazy or to distraction or worse.

But I do know right from wrong. There are a few simple facts that I know are true: I know that doing copious quantities of drugs has never gotten me anywhere besides rooms full of strangers in the basements of churches, drinking really bad coffee and saying, Thank you for sharing. I know that trying to be friends with ex-boyfriends causes nothing but irritation at best and serious damage at worst. I know that I feel a lot better when I have long, meandering conversations with God about the nature of my life and why it's not quite working out the way I wish it would. I know that I always do the best I can, and sappy as it sounds, I know it's good enough.

And I have loads of faith. All I can offer in the way of advice are a few hints about getting and muddling through along the way. The rest is your mess to make and clean up and enjoy. I hope you have fun. Because at the end of the day, having fun is the only real secret of life.

The
SECRET
of
LIFE

Always Ask

People have the power
The power to dream/to rule
to wrestle the earth from fools
PATTI SMITH
"People Have the Power"

This is the essence of life. This is the only reason to get out of bed in the morning. Every day is a new opportunity to ask more questions and see what happens. If you do nothing else with your day, at least make many inquiries and feel free to demand good and satisfying answers from the powers that be, or just from some slightly nervous human being who is a bit put off by your forthrightness. Be especially demanding of those people: They are the ones who are standing in your way, whether they mean to or not.

In fact, it is fair to say that whether it intends to or not, the whole world is conspiring to keep you silent; do not be party to this cabal.

This does not mean that you ought to make a nuisance or menace of yourself—it is only to say that it is important to wonder, and sometimes you might want to do this out loud. This does not mean you should go through life in a manic talking spree, but if something seems very wrong to you or, better still, if something seems just right, do not let the moment pass you by, unremarked, evanescent. I think what I am trying to say is something like, *seize the day*, only a little more fanciful.

If you don't ask you will never find out. You will never know if you could have had that great job, or if that guy was available, or who the rock group Tesla was named after (some scientist). You will never know the difference between an elk, a moose, a deer, and a reindeer (mostly size and antlers), or the meaning of the word *defenestrate* (look it up). You will never know if Freud's theories are more important than Marx's or, for that matter, if Einstein's ideas don't trump them both (debatable). You will go through life brain-dead, wondering why nothing ever seems to happen to you beyond day after dreary day.

The greatest party on earth, the really wild and rowdy one where all the happy people are, where all the beautiful people are—the one that all of us are sure we're not invited to, and all of us feel certain is going on right now, on the next block, within reach: you will never know how to find this party, how to get there, what shibboleth to use at the door, what to do once inside. You will miss out on all the fun just because you were afraid to ask.

Curious people are not always the happiest people, but they are never bored. They are the kind of people who amuse themselves while in the queue to renew their driver's license by getting the life story of the person in front of them, and they are the women who meet the men they are to marry on an intercontinental flight or walking out of the cinema or in any of those places where people are supposed to meet but only the brave and slightly crazy ever do. People are constantly falling in love with women who ask a lot of questions, because inquisitive types are comfortable enough with what they know to admit to what they don't—and because they are often provocateurs, which is always sexy.

Eat Dessert

*

> If I can't have too many truffles,
> I'll have no truffles.
> COLETTE

I have a dream that some day I will have a daughter who will believe she can eat what she wants, when she wants, without worrying about her thighs or her abs or her butt or the saggy batlike Hadassah arms that some women get at middle age. Maybe she won't even know the word *cellulite*.

Is this too much to expect? I think not. But in the meantime women can stubbornly refuse to succumb to the notion that food is the enemy. We can all join up with the Chocolate Cake Revolution (so far, I am the only member) and learn to love what is yummy once again. The fact is that if you really eat what you want when you want it and exercise three times a week like the experts say you should, you'll be fine. The whole offensive culture of dieting seems invented as yet another way to make women smaller and weaker—to make us become *less,* quite literally. The starving self symbolizes a diminishing person, and really we ought to strive to be *more,* to have more strength and muscle and inner resolve—which is what we get from working out or playing a sport, and what we lose when we live in hunger.

Even though models must be remarkably thin to mannequin clothes correctly—from a designer's perspective, the closer they come to resembling hangers, the better the dress will fall—most of us need not be concerned about how we'll appear on a runway or in fashion photographs. Those of us who are not Naomi or Shalom or Giscle must get off our imaginary catwalks and return to the land of flesh and blood, the sooner the better. Most of us need only worry about how we look in real life, which is not static, which allows our vitality and expressiveness to be part of our gorgeousness. The first step toward becoming this kind of living, breathing beauty is to eat your banana cream pie and cheesecake with great relish, to have your dessert like you believe you deserve it.

Men, by the way, find this trait very attractive, in contrast to vomitatious eating disorders, which no one finds appealing.

Don't Clear the Table at a Dinner Party Unless the Men Get Up to Help Too

*

Elegance is refusal.
COCO CHANEL

You know how it is. Friends are trying to be domestic and act grown up by having a bunch of people over for a meal. Invariably, the risotto will be too sticky, the salmon will be overcooked, the dill sauce will be too salty (don't ask), the salad will suffer from too many endives and too few tomatoes—but the effort will, of course, be the whole point. You will feel momentarily as mature as your parents were at your age—without having to feel *stuck* as they felt at almost every age. And to be appreciative and well mannered, between courses and at the end of the meal, you and others will get up to clear the table and help wash the dishes, because that's the right thing to do.

Now, as it happens, I have it on good authority from those who know about etiquette, that when you are a guest at somebody else's table, you not only need not offer to help, but in fact *should* let your hosts attend to all the post-repast cleaning. But because these good manners were formulated with assumptions of butlers and maids figured in—and presumptions of reciprocity that take for granted that all involved are willing and able to cook a passable meal they would wish to share with others—it is probably acceptable and desirable to help with the cleanup effort.

But *not* if the men don't. Cleanup tasks should not be gendered.

Do you want to know how you can change the whole world, one dinner table at a time? By holding a sit-in! By refusing to be helpful unless the men are!

Stay in your chair, savor a few more sips of your Merlot, finish the last spoonfuls of your melting orange-kumquat sorbet, and simply refuse to participate in a process that maintains the status quo of women serving men. In fact, even if the men *do* get up to bus tables and help load the dishwasher, you should just sit there and let them take care of it. It is your due. For thousands of years women have served men, and the alarm clock of history has at long last rung. This is just how it is, and ours is not to question why. It is time to let them have dishpan hands.

The revolution begins in the kitchen!

Have Opinions

✳

She has brought them to her senses
JONI MITCHELL
"Cactus Tree"

It's not a bad idea to be in-the-know and thoroughly opinionated about events occurring beyond your love life and immediate clique of friends. For one thing, it will give your mind something better to do than just be mad at ex-boyfriends and looking for a new one. But besides that, a woman who understands international—or even national—affairs is always sexy. And at this point in the time of mankind, there is simply no excuse: It is *irresponsible* not to have a cursory knowledge of the mess of the world, why it is messy, and why it is getting messier. If the best you can do is quote Bono's opinion—well, that puts you ahead of the person who can only manage to muster up Sheryl Crow's deep thoughts. If, at a dinner party, you can very quietly explain to some vulgar, outspoken man exactly why he has not a clue about what is going on in the Balkan states—never once raising your voice, always forcing everyone else to lean in a little bit closer to hear what you have to say—all the men at the table will be completely besotted with you.

But, of course, you should have loftier reasons for becoming conversant in, say, the subject of American electoral politics or the critical response to Philip Roth's latest novel or whether art still matters or if Russia will ever be economically viable. You shouldn't become well informed and full of moxie merely as a flirtation device.

Because, unfortunately, if your insights are all borrowed from cheat sheets and parroted from overheard chatter at the office watercooler, you will be found out. It is *very* easy to spot a charlatan. Somehow, even people who are ill informed and unenlightened themselves can tell whether it's all smoke and mirrors, or if you have genuine knowledge of whatever recondite topic you want to make the subject of your expertise and outrage.

How it is possible to become interested in politics and culture if you just aren't, I don't know. Perhaps it would be easier to learn to hold forth on this year's Oscar winners or last year's inductees into the Rock 'n' Roll Hall of Fame. The point is, no matter what you choose to be opinionated about, know your facts, lest you err on the side of alienating, rather than illuminating, your audience.

Be Gorgeous

✳

There are no ugly women, only lazy ones.
Helena Rubenstein

Obviously, you are born with what you're born with, and even plastic surgery can't change all that much (more on this subject later). But you *must* make the absolute most of what you have, you *must* present yourself to the world as the most delicious, enticing, and well-wrapped package you can possibly manage. This rule applies to men, women, teenagers, children, toddlers, and infants of all ages. (Sadly for some of us, it is when we are still babies that we will be the best dressed in all our lives, because we are often showered with adorable little outfits in our first years that are of a spectacular quality that we will never be able to afford or duplicate as adults; but that is that.) While *pretty* and *beautiful* are qualities that you cannot cultivate without a little help from the gods, *gorgeous* is actually available for the asking.

Now first, let's explain *pretty,* and give a few examples. Pretty is a demure loveliness, a hopelessly refreshing quality, a sweet healthy English-rose radiance without the Gorgon-ish fierceness and fright that true beauty can emit as a side effect. Pretty is adorable and warm: No matter what Jennifer Aniston does, she will always be the girl next door, she is just too damn pretty. (That Brad Pitt went from Gwyneth Paltrow, who is ethereal and etched like stone, to someone with such hardy, earthy good looks as Aniston is a sign that he has better taste in women than he does in choosing roles.) Cameron Diaz is, feature by feature, perhaps a beauty, but the parts she plays, most especially earlier in her career in *My Best Friend's Wedding* and *There's Something About Mary,* render her supremely pretty. Julia Roberts, particularly in *Pretty Woman,* is perhaps our best exemplar of prettiness. Of course, Ms. Roberts' supernatural smile and movie-star glow can make one mistake her for beautiful. Pretty multiplied geometrically can become beautiful. For instance, Audrey Hepburn was so, so pretty that she actually was beautiful.

Beautiful is sublime: Elizabeth Taylor's violet eyes, Sophia Loren's full-figured lips, Grace Kelly's elegance, Sharon Stone's iciness, Julie Christie's rosy cheeks, Deborah Harry's convex cheekbones. You only need be blessed with one such feature to be beautiful. Beautiful is forbidding and otherworldly, and often seems to come in inverse proportion to personal happiness, which is as good as any reason to thank your stars if you are not beautiful yourself.

You may not have any or all of the facets of beautiful or pretty, and heaven knows that you *can't* acquire them surgically—not even on Extreme Makeover—but you can try to present yourself to the outside world as if, for all they know, you might be Miss Universe. This does not mean you are supposed to apply pancake makeup and chartreuse eye shadow and fake lashes and tangerine-dream lipstick until you look like a drag queen or Christina Aguillera—or a drag queen dolled up as Christina Aguillera. This does not mean you are supposed to stand in front of the mirror primping and prodding yourself for hours each day until you develop excessive grooming disorder. (EGD is in fact an obsessive-compulsive syndrome found occasionally in maladjusted house cats, and involves tearing out clumps of hair, a behavior that is treated by keeping an inverted cone around the animal's neck for an extended period of time; this is not something you want to acquire yourself.) All it means is that you must pull yourself together before you leave the house—unless of course all you are doing is going for a jog, in which case a healthy glow will be all the loveliness that you will need.

The way to be gorgeous is to just make sure the basics are covered. Either you have long, flowing beautiful hair or you get an awesome cut. Do not dye, highlight, lowlight, or in any way alter your hair color yourself; if you must mortgage your house or find a better job in order to afford a good colorist, it is worth it. It will also last longer if done by expert hands. (I know from whence I speak: even when I was living on the Lower East Side of Manhattan, sharing a building with crackheads and their dealers, if I had to save rolls of pennies to afford it, I went to Madison Avenue for highlights, and I still believe it was one of the more worthwhile ways I spent my money at the time.) Have facials, massages, and all those other pampering things as often as you can, because if you do these things with regularity, you will start to feel it is your right to be treated right. And people who feel entitled are more likely to get what they want than those who meekly stand by in a chronic state of worthlessness.

Most women don't need more in the way of makeup than mascara and lipstick, and even if you are just running down the block to buy a newspaper and a pack of Marlboro Lights, I would suggest applying a little of these. This is not because you are likely to run into the man of your dreams en route—though who knows, stranger things have happened—it's just that I believe the very old-fashioned notion that if you do yourself up a bit, you will feel better, and therefore radiate vibes of pretty and beautiful, whether or not you actually are in possession of the real thing.

And besides—forgive me for sounding like my mother—but you owe the rest of the world the respect of a presentable presence. Life is icky enough without being confronted by your matted hair, your dots of Clearasil, your filthy T-shirt that you slept in that says "I'm with Stupid" over a tie-dye pattern. You may have to look at yourself like that in the mirror, but why should I and everyone else you cross paths with have to suffer? While I'm at it, may I suggest that if you have thick thighs, there is no reason to wear a mini skirt, and if you have a jiggly stomach, there is absolutely no need for low-rise jeans. If you can't avoid these sartorial mishaps for your own sake, then do it for everyone else's. Do it for the Gipper. Do it for world peace. Do it for God and country. But do take care to take care.

And in the course of taking care of yourself, somehow you will get better-looking. No one knows precisely how this alchemy works, but attending to your personal needs and wants and desires is more likely to prettify and beautify you than any kind of plastic surgery. This is just an axiom that you must accept without proof—just as for hundreds of years mathematicians accepted Fermat's Last Theorem without knowing at all why—because it simply is true. If that does not make sense to you, feel free to borrow my belief: I myself believe that I am about ten times prettier than I actually am. By dint of sheer will-power, I have managed to convince many people of this.

There is no way to avoid discussing plastic surgery in this context, though I would just as soon skip it. I really believe that if you want to have a face-lift to decelerate the signs of aging, that is quite understandable; but altering the features on your face is fighting against nature in a vain battle. In fact, I would argue that people who achieve acceptance of their God-given qualities almost always seem better-looking than those who have handed over their faces to the surgeon's knife. Consider Princess Diana, whose angular and slightly smashed-in nose was part of her beauty. (I realize, of course, that teenagers who feel they really need nose jobs—and who indeed have outsize, bulbous arrays of bone and cartilage in the middle of their faces—might be a surgery segment all their own, but that's a whole other issue.)

One of the interesting ways to recognize that surgery can make a clear difference to an individual feature, but can do very little to change the face as a whole, is to consider the looks of great beauties who have had, for instance, rhinoplasties. No one knows for certain if Michelle Pfeiffer had her nose done, but many magazine articles about Hollywood and cosmetic surgery have shown old photographs of her alongside new ones, and it seems pretty obvious that her nostrils look a bit more pinched, that the bone in the center is a bit smoother and narrower. But so what? She was already beautiful in the first place, and a slight imperfection that probably was worsened by the camera (which is why it needed to be fixed) is removed in the second place. All the same, no matter how many nose jobs you have, you are still not going to look like Michelle Pfeiffer. Likewise, it's hard to figure out why Cher has had so much surgery on her face, which was exotically beautiful all along. Nevertheless, no matter how many alterations she has done—cheekbones and nose and eyes and whatever else from the neck down—Cher still looks like Cher. You don't.

So best start believing and therefore being gorgeous, regardless of what you need to do to convince yourself you are, because it's the only trick that really works.

Consider the fates of a few famous and visually unexceptional or unbecoming women. Patti Smith, who seems to have embraced *deficient* grooming disorder as a lifestyle, still can be said to always get the boy. Playwright and actor Sam Shepard, at the time the beauty of underground drama and today still a ridiculously rugged and handsome and laconic man, spent a few good years madly in love with Patti. At some point, in some sense, Ms. Smith also shacked up with Robert Mapplethorpe, the famously gay photographer. And though no one knows the precise

nature of the relationship, it is interesting to specu-
late on the possibility that Mapplethorpe abandoned
his sexual preference for a time because he was so in
love with her. Later on, Patti Smith settled down in
Michigan with Fred "Sonic" Smith of the MC5, who
is certainly a good catch in someone's notion of cool.
Patti Smith seems to have managed all this, quite
possibly, without ever shaving her underarms or without ever combing her hair. Obviously, by her own
standard, Patti Smith feels gorgeous.

Exene Cervenka, singer of the Los Angeles punk
band X and alleged poet, is also a ratty-looking little
woman. I mean, I have seen the band in concert, and
Exene projects such unpleasant uncleanness that you
do not need to be near the stage to feel it. But somehow she was married to bandmate John Doe, who is
a big hulking beautiful blue-eyed guy. After the divorce, she married Viggo Mortensen, who has classic
movie-star good looks, and who played obscenely
sexy wife-stealers in both *A Perfect Murder* (opposite
Gwyneth Paltrow) and *A Walk on the Moon* (with Di-
ane Lane) before hitting it big in the *Lord of the Rings*
trilogy. Personally, I would cross eight lanes of moving traffic for the mere *possibility* of meeting Viggo; he
is *that* hot. But with both these men, it's not just their

male beauty that moves me; it is a quality of gentleness, and what can only be called "real-man" stature, that makes me wonder why both are not world famous, as they should be. Nevertheless, Exene Cervenka has been with both of them, and I have been with neither one.

The best-known ugly-gorgeous woman at the moment is Courtney Love. She has never been shy about confessing to her various aesthetic surgeries, which perhaps by the common standard improved her looks. Personally, I prefer her the old way, before Versace and CAA entered her life, when she was clearly odd-looking. Because Kurt Cobain, at that point, was the best catch in the world of rock music. And the woman he let grab him was really kind of awful—yucky to look at, screechy to listen to. There was a moment there when Courtney showed the world what gorgeous really means, when she made it clear that it was bigger than beauty itself. And then she was all manicured and yoga-fied, a Hollywood gal taking meetings and having lunch. And then it all went wrong. It had to. Smaller nose, bigger boobs— Courtney might have built a better blonde, but that's all it is. She used to be gorgeous. Now she's just plastic.

These three aforementioned women, and many

more we've never heard of, are inexplicable phenomena. They always get the guy because they are simply cool and hot and full of exciting energy. There are always a few such women running around that the rest of us must enviously contend with. Nothing you can do can get that certain "it" thing.

Have Pets

✳

I don't believe in hatred anymore
I hate to think of how I felt before
EDIE BRICKELL
"Love Like We Do"

And if you have allergies, find a way to overcome them, because animals are awesome.

As will be discussed in advice about dealing with ex-boyfriends, you will find the loyalest, kindest, sweetest companion not at a singles bar, but at an animal shelter. The easiest animals to take into your household are kittens or cats, who don't need to go for pedestrian outings several times a day, and seem to be born with an a priori understanding of what a litter box is for. Also, it's easy to have more than one of them, since their needs are so minuscule. In fact, I would recommend getting at least two felines from the get-go so that they can keep each other company during the long hours that you may be out of the house during the day or night or on long weekends. So long as you leave them with enough food, cats can fend for themselves for several days at a time, but they do get lonely.

Until he died in the summer of 2003, I had only one car—as a result of various apartment problems and such when I first moved to New York after college—and I felt so dreadfully guilty when I left him alone for any extended period of time. When I went away for more than a couple of days, I always found someone to house-sit for me, to keep him company as he so generously did for me all his life. Zap died at age fourteen. I was holding him. The last thing I told him was that knowing him had been the greatest privilege of my life. Which sounds crazy— unless you have had a pet yourself.

Dogs are, of course, a major maintenance project, but how nice to have a pet that is portable, that you can take with you anywhere. Dogs are notoriously loyal creatures, with an acute sensitivity that is comforting in hard times and just plain exhilarating when things are going well. They also have astonishing precognition about who will fuck you over, and they have an alarming ability to show teeth to the enemy. (Ex-lovers beware.) So if you have the wherewithal to provide the necessary care—and let's just say it up front, we are talking about a serious commitment—I would go to the pound and adopt one immediately. Do not pass Go, do not collect two hundred dollars, just go to the shelter. Because, besides everything else, men in particular, but people in general, think a woman who can handle a dog is pretty damn cool. If she can take care of such a demanding creature, most likely she can take pretty good care of herself.

And she also *has* to keep her priorities in order. She can't stay out all night, because the dog needs to be walked and generally attended to. She will not be able to drop everything, abandon her knitting, stop going to the gym, forget to call her friends, give up stamp-collecting, and allow her house to turn into a dirty heap of dishes and debris—she cannot let herself go to pot because she has a higher calling; she has to care for her dog, and that is that. Everybody—but most especially boyfriend types—appreciates a woman who attends to her responsibilities. I found Augusta, a three-month-old all black border-collie mix, a month after my cat died. I've been walking her ever since. I used to do many things with my time, but now I just walk the dog. Make no mistake: Having a dog is devotion absolutely. It is the best thing ever—and it's everything altogether.

If you are not up to being a good dog owner, if you are still doing cocaine until five in the morning and falling asleep on a duvet on the floor after maybe or maybe not having sex with somebody or other, don't get a dog. Stick with cats. Also, if you are not prepared to meticulously train your canine friend, forget about it. Dogs who were not well housebroken or overindulged or mistreated early on turn into annoying nightmarish creatures who will ruin your chance of ever having a successful dinner party or of entertaining a gentleman caller à deux.

But the cat option remains viable for even the most fucked up among us. (I know from whence I speak.) Many unenlightened fools associate cat ownership with pathetic, chronic spinster status. They envision you as an old maid wearing purple and an oversized brooch, sitting on your easy chair while an uncountable tribe of tabbies and calicoes and the like overrun the living room.

This frequently exploited image of the typical cat

owner is just a socially imposed fabrication meant to make you feel bad and ashamed of something that is perfectly right and good. This is sexism at its most absurd. Plenty of men and married people have cats, and adopting a couple of them will not make you into a deranged dowager. Anybody who has ever visited Key West in Florida, and has taken a tour of Ernest Hemingway's residence there, can tell you that it is a house full of cats. "Papa" invited them in when he was alive, and they have stayed there and fruitfully multiplied in the years since his death. While Hemingway may have been as loony as it gets, he was also thought to be—by himself and others—as macho as it gets. His brood of cats did not make him a sissy, and it certainly did not turn him into a peculiar old lady. Do not be done in by what others misguidedly think.

Save Yourself

✳

> You look like the perfect fit
> For a girl in need of a tourniquet
> AIMEE MANN
> "Save Me"

Don't expect some guy to save you. Do not sit around thinking that all would be perfect if only you had a boyfriend to catch your pained tears and hold a Kleenex around your nostrils while you blow your nose. Because, unfortunately, that is not how it works. The way it works is that the great guy of your dreams does not show up until things finally *are* perfect, until you yourself have tended to the delicate garden that is your life. (Forget perfect—just shoot for well and solid enough.) And this is a lucky thing, because when you are down in the dumps, the last thing you need is a man.

Most men who are sane and employed do not want to repair your broken pieces and make an even-keeled jigsaw puzzle out of you. But if you should happen to find yourself a personal Jesus at some local bar, and he wants nothing more than to heal your childhood traumas and absorb all your pain and spend long hours of daylight with the curtains drawn, in bed with you, mostly *not* having sex, do not mistake the initial warm and fuzzy feeling for true love. Accept it for the folie à deux it will surely become, run for the hills as fast as you can, and make a point of seeking out professional help (see next entry) for whatever it is that makes you think a man can save you.

In general, love has never rescued a person who has not first reclaimed herself. I have a friend, in this case it happens to be a guy, whose life was floundering in every which way. He went from menial job to meaningless job for years, working as an unpaid intern at a low-rent cable television outfit and as a copy editor for the house organ of some right-minded environmental organization. He was a researcher at a magazine about birds—and he got fired. He moved from New York to Los Angeles to Vermont to Amsterdam to New York again. He wrote two unpublished (and unpublishable) novels. He went from one short-lived and inauspicious and inexplicable relationship to another.

Finally, somewhere along the line, he found within himself either the wherewithal or the disgust or perhaps even the courage to *just get a job.* Any job. He was not looking for a career opportunity, because by that time he simply needed to do something that would pay the rent so that he could stay in one place long enough to get settled and centered. The most lucrative setups he could find were entry-level positions on Wall Street, which seemed a hopeless last attempt at hope at the time. Amazingly enough, it turned out that he was good at his work, that he actually even had an affinity for it, which everyone at the office took note of. When his boss was fired, he was promoted to that position, and the bonuses and offers keep coming along. He was even poached by another firm. His annual earnings are now in the millions— after only a few years on the job. Meanwhile, in his newly secure state, he found a girlfriend he is crazy for, and he's bought a town house where they can maybe live happily ever after.

Let me assure you that this friend was a complete

loser for several years there. Believe me, he was truly pathetic.

But by taking minute steps toward winnerdom, he eventually got all of life's happy rewards, day by day, piece by piece. What people whom I don't like very much call karma is a real, terrestrial energy that works when you work with it. If you do the right things and act as if you believe there is a modicum of hope for you, soon whatever force that controls the universe will begin to smile upon your little life and let it bloom.

Use All Available Resources

*

The hardest part is knowing I'll survive
EMMYLOU HARRIS
"Boulder to Birmingham"

When something is wrong, and is fixable through professional intervention—be it a clogged sink, a mouse in the house, or a lengthy bout with depression—don't idly complain to your friends until they want to kill you. Unless you are ninety years old and on your deathbed, there is probably *something* you can do about your problems. (And when you are old and in pain, when someone offers you a morphine drip, for heaven's sake, take it!) Try acupuncture and yoga and Pilates and lifting weights. Get psychiatric help or any other kind of help that's available. Call an exterminator. Do not be puritanical about it. Let the M.D.s and Ph.D.s help you solve your problem so that you don't become hatefully everyone else's problem. It is your friends' and family's proper job to support you lovingly throughout your life, but—as is the case with any man—not to save you.

And, as a general rule, do not be any more of a pain in the ass to others than is absolutely necessary, for reasons of etiquette *and* of expediency. Boy problems, job difficulties, the day-to-day nuisances of life: These are appropriate items to bring to friends. Ideally, of course, your lives will be so wonderful and trouble-free that you will only discuss new theories of the nature of evil, what quarks actually are, if Kevin Costner still has a viable career, or whether you believe there is a gene for homosexuality. Not that friendships should model themselves on the Oxford Debating Society, but a certain amount of abstract thought and engagement with the outside world is a good thing.

The situation you want most to avoid is what I call task-oriented relationships. This happens when you feel that the only way you can sense another's devotion or interest is by getting him to help you with something—setting up your stereo or uncorking a bottle of wine or walking you home late at night. It's not that you can't get a friend—or more likely, a boyfriend—to help you in these ways; it's just that it becomes patently obvious to the helpmate that this is a way of testing his commitment or exacting a false sense of devotion, because you tell yourself he wouldn't be so helpful if he didn't care at least an eensy-weensy bit. Guys feel this manipulation quite acutely, and they don't much like it. If he's interested in you, you can have dinner or sex or whatever together without getting him to change all your light-bulbs just to prove to yourself that he is becoming part of the household. If you're a big girl, you're big enough to get a stepladder or to call in the janitor.

And this is not just in the case of male-female relationships. My mother drives me absolutely crazy by asking me to come over for lunch on a Saturday afternoon to help her move her black lacquer table from one end of the dining room to the other. Or she needs help buying a present for the rabbi's new baby. Or she wants me to see the Day-Glo orange outfit she just bought, in case it is too garish. Of course, the obligatory setting-the-clock-on-the-VCR had to fit in there somewhere. And I am happy to do these things for her. But I resent her need to find excuses for having a relationship. After all, I don't need a reason to see her—I love her, and, more to the point, I like her, and she should know that. The pretenses she comes up with make me want to see her less rather than more.

On the whole, relationships that are run under duress are to be avoided like the plague. If you have a friend who only calls you up to say that there are black waves crashing in her head and she is scared to death and maybe even thinks she is dying, that is not fair. You are not a psychiatric professional. Similarly, don't lure a guy up to your apartment with promises of a beetle that needs to be stamped on unless you have been involved for a long time and he knows this is a legitimate fear. Don't use it as an excuse to call a guy whom you slept with three days ago and have not heard from. In such a ghastly situation—I am referring to the beetle, not the postsex silence—a courageous old friend is the appropriate one to call.

But above all, beyond any of the other ways that you might be using friends for inappropriate purposes—even worse than, say, asking a good buddy to assuage your undiagnosed schizophrenia (which is at least an understandable mistake)—do not *under any circumstances* ask anyone that you care for to help you move from one apartment to another. In fact, the simple rule is: *If you can't afford a mover, you can't afford to move.* Asking friends to lift large boxes is *not* okay. Asking them to then carry them up or down several flights of stairs—and if you are resorting to getting help from friends, you are also probably moving from one to another fifth story walk up—is further unacceptable. This is not what friends are for. They are for movie dates and drinks after work, not lugging. They can bring a casserole to help you settle in, keep you company while you pack and unpack, but physical labor is for paid help only. (You can pay your friends, but that's a bit déclassé.)

Exceptions are at college, when your comrades are allowed to help you carry your books and beanbag chairs from one dormitory room to another, and taking people out for a few rounds of beer in the aftermath is okay. And had I not actually done this myself a few times in my undergraduate days, I would consider this absolutely verboten.

Have a Cleaning Person Come in as Often as You Can Afford

✳

I would prefer not to.
HERMAN MELVILLE
"Bartleby, the Scrivener"

Which is to say: Make your life as easy as possible, because no matter what your mother told you, it is no virtue to do menial, miserable tasks if you can pay someone else to. To take the advice of Agatha Christie, surely one of the most prolific woman writers ever (and obviously someone who did not waste her time scouring the floors): "Never do anything yourself that others can do for you."

This rule is obviously a corollary to the previous law about employing all available resources. The simple principle comes down to this: You should not be a spoiled brat, you should not throw tantrums to get others to do your bidding, but you should, by honest means, avoid any daily drudgery that you possibly can. You should find some sort of way to earn enough money to provide for yourself and all your basic needs—and at least in my case, the "basic needs" tend to be rather elaborate.

If you are doing something worthy with your life, like helping to end hunger in the Sudan or trying to resettle ethnic Albanians, you are probably not reading this book, and, more to the point, you probably have pared down the necessities to not much more than running water, a faulty heating system, and the occasional purchase of a Chanel nail polish. Or, perhaps, you have a hefty trust fund. Either way, I say more power to you, even though this unfortunately means that you will probably have to scrub your own tub.

Have a Job, Have Your Own Money, Support Yourself

*

*People call me a feminist whenever
I express sentiments that differentiate me
from a doormat or a prostitute.*
REBECCA WEST

I might as well be saying, *have a brain*. That's how crucial this dictum is. It is the one and only irrefutable rule, one of those absolute truths whose merits have been demonstrated time and again—mostly by way of the negative example of what happens to girls who can't, won't, or don't earn their own living.

Let's make sure that I am making myself perfectly clear. You can do anything you want with anyone you want; you can shack up with a man, get married to a man, have children with a man, spend the rest of your loving days and happy nights with a man. But you must *never* be beholden to him for money. You must never become a dependent—leave that role to your offspring.

Because he will start to hate you for abandoning the sassy spirit you once had, and for turning what was once love into a ball and chain. And you will despise yourself for not mattering to the world—after all, in a capitalist society, if you don't have an income you don't matter. (That is not a value judgment—it is just the truth.) You will become a human parasite, supported by your husband mostly out of a sense of guilt. The vicious cycle of neediness and control will brutally inflict itself upon what was once a loving partnership; you will be bored, and your husband will be bored-er. And then if you don't, in some premenstrual state of infuriation, leave him, he will, in some middle-aged phase of infatuation, leave you faster than you can say Porsche 944.

By that time, you can only hope that you might have found some dalliances of your own, a bit of love in the afternoon on the sly. The arrival of the Federal Express delivery man may become the highlight of your day. Best-case scenario, you are Catherine Deneuve in *Belle de Jour:* You find prostitution preferable to housewifery.

But let us consider the income imperative from a positive perspective. Let's, for a moment, not fixate on husbands who disappear in the night—because there is more to it. Girls who pay their own rent don't have to be nice. They don't have to be mean either— and most likely they will be kind and considerate, because these traits are easier to cultivate when you don't feel trapped in a miserable relationship for financial need, or indebted to some man who is just a lifeline to Prada or Pottery Barn or even plain old groceries.

Of course, the dependent woman feels like a thousand pounds of dead weight to the breadwinning man, and in this manner the nature of their whole relationship is perverted into banking transactions, the love itself either gone or buried beneath a heap of need and obligation. It was from this kind of miserable affair of give-and-take that the women's movement emerged. Make no mistake, women would not have started having consciousness-raising groups in their cellars if they were happy homemakers. As we

all know, a happy person would do just about anything to avoid attending a long, emotional gathering
where one woman confesses to a bloody illegal abor-
tion in 1952, and another one admits that she has no
idea what foreplay is, and another reports that when
she was in college, she was so bold and she had lots of
audacious thoughts and dreams, but now her whole
life is laundry and dirty dishes, and she has no idea
how this happened to her. People do not involve
themselves in these kinds of misery marathons unless they are thoroughly fed up with life such as it is,
and I don't know how many reminders it will take before we get that straight.

A brief history lesson for those who missed out
the first time. Here is how feminism got its start:
There were many bright and bored women living in
suburbs, playing mah-jongg to pass the time, and ex-
periencing the occasional bit of domestic excitement
when one of their children fell off his bicycle and
needed his knee dressed and bandaged. Eventually,
they found themselves with kids old enough to care
for themselves, and these teenagers would get snap-
pish when their mothers were underfoot or tried to
interfere in their little lives—but what else were these

women to do? So many of them went crazy and got addicted to Valium and Librium, and some of them joined up with the nascent women's movement.

Some of them discovered that they were lesbians and never knew it. Others found themselves attracted to younger men who introduced them to the joys of cunnilingus. But most of them tried to keep their family lives intact while opening themselves up to new, stimulating, and ecstatic possibilities.

Feminism saved these women's lives. It saved your life too, and if you don't know that, you are reading the wrong book. I am not advocating that women abdicate their maternal roles—though I would like to see fathers pick up some of the slack, which would be better for both the parents *and* the children. All I am saying is that a mind needs to be occupied by real and valuable and nourishing activities. If you do nothing all day but window-shop and go for pedicures, you will end the day with nice feet and an empty head.

If, right about now, you are saying to yourself something about feeling exhausted and disgusted and having a job you hate, one that you would gladly leave if you could afford to, then you have another problem entirely. You have to find something enjoyable to do, you have to return to college or take vocational courses, or do whatever you can to make gainful employment tolerable.

Because there is a nice part to all of this. It does get better. I am told that women who learn to take care of themselves have a pretty good chance of meeting a man who is similarly self-sufficient. And then—! —an amazing thing actually might happen: You just might be able to take care of each other.

Embrace Fanaticism

*

He not busy being born
Is busy dying
BOB DYLAN
"Its Alright, Ma
(I'm Only Bleeding)"

Learn to love things other than boys.
Women must learn how to be complete
nutcases and crazily committed to ideas, theology,
interests—anything. We must be positively bonk-
ers about something other than men. Consider this
analogy: During World War II, Winston Churchill
spoke of the importance of the government's contin-
ued subsidy of the arts, explaining that there was no
point sending men out to fight if there was no civiliz-
ation worth saving—and worthy of returning home

to. Likewise, the point of this whole sexual revolution was to give women fuller lives; it was not so that we could grimly labor to earn only three-quarters of what men do, and then come home to nothing but housework and screaming children to attend to.

If women had the kinds of consuming passions that men seem to—be it watching football or playing golf or a weekly poker game or drinking with the boys—that they could absolutely and completely be sure not to allow *a single fucking thing to get in the way of,* we would do more to assert our rights than we do by, for instance, filing a complaint with the personnel department when the boss says, *Hey, baby, nice butt.* Because, righteous as it is to call the sleaze who is your superior on his sexually harassing behavior, it's not particularly fun; in fact, it is probably a rather tedious, tiresome procedure, which is why so many women don't bother.

But insisting upon doing something you love no matter what—well, that makes a woman a creature of enjoyment and indulgence and, frankly, a certain kind of self-sufficiency that is positively liberating. It is empowering to say *no,* but it is a great deal more pleasurable to say *yes*—and to have things to say yes to besides some man. Unfortunately, for those of us above the age of consent, it's hard to change habits of the heart. As it happens, the younger generation has started to learn a trick that men have long known: Athletics are the best way to ignore the rest of the world and invest yourself completely in the here and now, in what is present and perfect and right in front of you. In the United States, by the end of the twentieth century, 2.5 million girls competed on high school teams, up from 300,000 in the seventies. Soccer has never made much headway in any American professional league, which has made it an opportune playing field for women to make a mark in—which is why our women's team won the 1999 World Cup while our men's team barely got beyond the first round in 1998. Studies have shown that girls who play sports have higher self-esteem (whatever that means), wait longer to have sex, and choose to have fewer partners. (Okay, so they don't sound like the funnest lot, but looking back on my teenage years, I'd give anything to have been a little less boy crazy, so maybe this is a good thing.)

But that aside, I would argue that a woman is more likely to put the kibosh on her manhandling, leering boss if she has lots of things she likes to do, because there is something about loving life and yourself and your enthusiasms too much that makes it hard to put up with any idiot's crap. And the people most likely to be in possession of that quality known as joie de vivre are people who have insane interests, consuming passions, constant sources of enjoyment that do not depend on the approval of others. "Be drunken, always. That is the point; nothing else matters," wrote Charles Baudelaire, a man who understood too well what it meant to give oneself over to life. "Drunken with what? With wine, with poetry or with virtue, as you please. But be drunken." And women must learn what is meant by these lines, what it means to be besotted with something other than some useless bloke.

Unless, of course, that useless bloke is Bob Dylan or Bruce Springsteen or some other genius of popular, populist art who comes up with lines and lyrics and chord progressions worth committing to memory. Why is it that not only are most musicians male, but even most serious *fans* are men? In high school, girls like the bands that their boyfriends like, and usually not even that much. Perhaps one of the reasons I do so much prefer *High Fidelity* to *Bridget Jones's Diary* is that Nick Hornby's Rob, pathetic schlemiel though he may be—completely commitment-phobic and puerile as a newborn—is still a devoted music fan; he's crazy for something other than his own neuroses. I myself have always felt that my life was saved by rock and roll, and I am baffled about why other women don't tend to have deposited their own desperation into such an obvious receptacle. I understand that it is the loser teenage boy mentality that is required to exact the kind of masturbatory devotion to guitar practice alone in your room that accounts for the lack of a female Jimi Hendrix, but why are there not more female Jimi Hendrix *fans* (not to be confused with groupies, another prefeminist proposition)?

And for all the complaints about feminists not getting behind Monica Lewinsky a few years back because of their loyalty to President Clinton, should we not be more concerned that the wiretapping Linda Tripp actually has some forty hours of the nubile, labile intern in an obsessional blather over Bill? Would it not have been better had these two at least nominally adult women occasionally talked about, say, our policy toward NATO or the failing Asian economy or any of the many topics that might be of interest to two people employed by the United States government? Often it seems to me that it is in this seemingly innocent and certainly silly situation—and not in its dealings with, say, date rape—that feminism reveals its failures. Because somehow forty years of the women's movement has not, for the most part, taught us to keep our eyes on the ball and not get distracted by trivial obsessions. Even the most serious and sturdy among us seem to be only one man away from being reduced to mashed potatoes.

This is not good. And to a certain extent, there is nothing any of us can do about it. But we must at least try to fight off this tendency to drop everything just because a guy you just met happens to look like Cary Grant. We must fight the good fight. We must make our lives as full and fulfilling and heavenly as possible. We must learn to have more fun.

If you still don't understand why you must have hobbies or take up a sport or read a newspaper, just consider how many activities of that type men engage in: From the most interesting and dashing gentleman to the dopiest and dullest loser, they all have some spectator sport that they are crazy for. Watching athletic activities while wives and girlfriends become bored "football widows" would seem a likely way to alienate your loved ones, but men don't mind, apparently, disappearing into television and leaving women and the world at large behind. In *Fever Pitch*, Nick

Hornby discusses men's ability to completely immerse themselves in football viewing, admitting that as a result, "they become repressed, they fail in their relationships with women, their conversation is trivial and boorish, they find themselves unable to express their emotional needs, they cannot relate to their children, and they die alone and miserable. But, you know, what the hell?" Somehow, unlike Bridget Jones, Hornby is not afraid of having his carcass half-eaten by a German shepherd.

At least football, a word used to describe a completely different game on this side of the ocean (though I often believe that the reason both European soccer and American football are called by the same name is to allow there to be one word that universally describes something that annoys all women), looks to us to be possibly fun. But men also take up sports that seem bizarrely pointless. Fly-fishing, for instance. This is an activity that involves some deeply meditative attempts to get into the minds of trout, and trick them out of the water, catch them, and throw them back in. On enough psilocybin, I think that many women could enjoy watching (and even playing) football; but I know of no drug that would make me disappear into fly-fishing country for several days, camping out among the grizzly bears, never being able to shampoo my hair, enjoying all the discomforts of nature just so that I could catch those floppy creatures and then throw them back out into the river to contend with the remainder of their piscine existence with tongue piercings they did not ask for. Contrary to what many men have explained to me about the sublime possibilities provided by 808 different kinds of bait, I have no doubt that my delight in spending three hours roaming through the cosmetics department of Bloomingdale's is still far more beautiful.

I mention this last personal passion because I truly believe that makeup, along with fashion, is hardly a harmful fascination. Even Naomi Wolf now concedes that lipstick is not the enemy. And I do think one can enjoy indulging in beauty absolutely for its own sake, as pleasure qua pleasure, boy-bait not an issue at all. But in excess, such concern is not merely vain but dangerously narcissistic—which is the same problem of obsessing over some man: You may think that you are thinking about *him,* but really you are thinking about yourself *via* him, which is not only ugly and unhealthy, but also a hellish path to an ugly and unhealthy relationship.

This is how women get themselves into trouble. Women who have better things to do than be obsessive stay out of trouble. So just find a way to become fanatical about something, just for fun. Take an interest in horse racing, or read Proust's *Remembrance of Things Past* in its entirety, or invest in the stock market, or learn to ski at a late age. The list of possibilities goes on and on. It is easy to develop interests—they are called that because they are *interesting*. Even boring people have been known to get excited about this or that thing—and they soon discover that the only reason they were boring is that they were bored.

See Lots of Movies

✳

*I was asked something about
genius, inspiration. Well, of course.
Without them, we're nothing.*
TERENCE MCNALLY
Master Class

Movies are surely among the easiest things to become fascinated with and fanatical about. With almost no effort at all, you can get yourself absolutely crazy about the films of Martin Scorsese or Max Ophuls or Robert Altman or Woody Allen or Bernardo Bertolucci or anyone with an Italian last name. If you are looking for a way to get your mind off your mind, movies are a good start.

And in general, entertain yourself as much as possible—read books, watch television, listen to music, follow every titillating fact of public scandals (but do be selective about which ones you choose to get caught up in). Be sure to go to the theater and attend exhibitions also. (Of course, not if you find these activities oppressive and dull, but that is another problem altogether.) Try to be, as one of my college professors would say, engagé.

After all, at the end of the day, culture, or whatever you want to call it, is pretty much all we humans have beyond our daily bread. In fact, the only thing that really separates us from the beasts of the jungles and savannahs of the world—besides, I suppose, that we have built missiles that almost guarantee our eventual self-destruction—is that we can play the clarinet, we can paint a starry night, we can compose an opera and write a sonnet. And on the subject of sonnets, if the only thing you know of Shakespeare dates back to when you were forced to read *Romeo and Juliet* in school at age twelve, you might want to remedy that. Contrary to common belief, Shakespeare's plays are easy to read, even relaxing; they are certainly not a chore.

I know what I am prescribing might sound a bit like a program of cultural boot camp, but actually it is meant to be quite the opposite. Because the more time you spend at the cinema or with a good page-turner, the more you will discover that *you are not alone*. You'll find out that your emotional life, however scary it seems to you when you are home alone with a bottle of Chianti on a Saturday night, is actually rather common. The more you read and attend and absorb of the available media, the less strange you will feel, and the more able you will be to achieve some measure of self-acceptance. All of the arts will do you the simple service of denying your unique misery. The power of great art is in its ability to deliver perspective, and the best of it has a specificity that is so trenchant that what is personal becomes universal.

Take *Blue*, the Joni Mitchell album from 1971, for example. It is an intimate and intense cycle of songs, telling stories of sorrow and heartbreak and ache that go deep down to the bone. *Blue* is one of the most revealing albums of this era, and Ms. Mitchell herself has said that she felt brutally vulnerable when she recorded it, as if her skin were made of sheer shrink-wrap, and everyone could see inside of her. This soul-stripped album, with its singular emotional ardor, would seem to suit only those people whose life experiences are identical to Joni's. But *Blue* has in fact sold millions of copies since its release, and most of the people who bought it have not used it as a sound track for an evening of wrist-slitting. The success of *Blue* indicates that many people indeed feel as bad as Joni did when she wrote and recorded that album; but it also means that many stable, steady people have their difficult moments when nothing but Joni's high-pitched voice and eccentric guitar tunings will do. Which means that all the despair and depression that you experience in the loneliest moments of life can even be comprehensible to, let's say, a drunken frat boy who bought *Blue* when he was still sensitive and fragile and sweet.

The great thing I have found about being completely immersed in movies and books and all that other stuff is that no matter what happens in the world or in my life, I am always aware that nothing that goes on now has not already been covered by the Bard or the Bible. O. J. Simpson's murder extravaganza was pretty much anticipated by *Othello*. President Clinton's sexual compulsion and the damage it has done have a precedent in the story of King David and Bathsheba.

History continually repeats itself, first as tragedy then as comedy, and thank God for that.

And while you are busy in pursuit of a liberal arts education, why not eliminate schlock from your life? Why not stop wasting your time watching dumb movies? And by dumb, I don't mean big thrilling science-fiction blockbusters like *Star Wars*. I don't mean funny and moving popular comedies like *The Wedding Singer*. I don't mean ingeniously offensive stuff like *South Park*. I don't mean movies that star Tom Cruise and involve Navy pilots or race-car drivers, because Tom Cruise is pretty spectacular in whatever he does, and don't try to tell me different. I don't mean a big sappy mess of a movie like *Forrest Gump*, because if something gets ridiculously popular like that, you want to be in on the conversation, you don't want to be the only one who can't argue its merits.

The sorts of movies to stay away from are really not that hard to categorize: the latest Sandra Bullock vehicle, almost any movie that claims to be a thriller and has the word "instinct," "fatal," or "fear" in its title, most movies that cast Sharon Stone against type, most movies that cast Demi Moore at all (there's a reason she was hiding in Idaho for all those years), any overgrown disaster like *Terminator 3* or, for that matter, anything with Arnold Schwartzenegger that postdates 1992. If you can't stay away from sequels, at least avoid the third installment—even *Godfather III* was tortuous and tortured, and that's a film series whose second part was at least as good as the first. Don't rent videotapes of movies to watch at home if they weren't worth seeing in the theater six months ago. Don't be scared of subtitles: The movies of Kieślowski, Almodóvar, Truffaut, and so many others simply defy language.

Above all, don't be afraid of black-and-white films from the thirties, forties, and fifties. Few movies are as sexy as *Double Indemnity*, as thrilling as *The Third Man*, or as hot as *Touch of Evil*. James Cagney pretty much invented cool in *White Heat*, and Veronica Lake simply was cool in *This Gun for Hire*. The hep-cat scenes in *Sweet Smell of Success*, the blonde and brunette mystery of Kim Novak in *Vertigo*, the great flirtation between Bogey and Bacall in *To Have and Have Not*—these are cinematic wonders that you don't want to miss. I am not prescribing these guidelines in a medicinal fashion—these movies will not make you a cleverer or better person. They are just great viewing fun, and one's life will not be complete without them. (Actually, they probably *will* make you a cleverer and better person, but just pretend you are in it strictly for kicks.)

Try to Know What the Kids are Up To

*

There is no new thing under the sun.
ECCLESIASTES 1:9

Let's face it: You will grow old no matter how much Retin-A you slather on at night, no matter how many alpha- and beta-hydroxy acids there are in your moisturizer, and no matter how many vitamin pills and youth sera and raw vegetables you eat each day. And you will start to wonder how it is that teenyboppers and their assorted idols seem so much stupider/louder/more obnoxious than you and yours ever were. You will think that when you were young, you had ideology and hope, but today's kids just have idiocy and despair. Worst of all, they seem to like it like that. You will tell yourself that, somehow, if you really think about it, Duran Duran was meaningful and 'N Sync is not. You will remember a time when MTV was—yes—*subversive*.

Once you are done being disgusted with their "music," you will then be baffled by the aesthetic choices of the younger generation—I certainly am. You will find green hair and eyebrow rings and those bovine nose hooks that they seem to like increasingly repulsive and hideous. You will wonder why it is that these teenagers want to make themselves look so ugly, why they can't just wear the belly-baring stretch skirts and layers of black gauze and armfuls of black rubber bracelets like Madonna taught us to do. You will have no idea why all the boys want to be a *mack daddy,* and you will be dumbfounded by the allure of Special K—the horse tranquilizer that gives users a special sense of being trapped in a dark dungeon— and you will be even more astonished by whatever cool drug the rave kids come up with next.

In other words, you will be out of it just like your mother is out of it. You will listen to Fleetwood Mac and Kate Bush and—heaven help you—Enya on a regular basis. You will occasionally pull out *Never Mind the Bollocks* just to prove to yourself that it was not always thus, that once upon a time you were a kid who wanted to destroy passersby. But essentially, you will not have a clue. Your adolescent kids will think you are pathetic, and you will find that you don't trust anyone under thirty. Styles come and bands go, and hemlines go up and down; only the generation gap persists.

But that does not mean you can't at least know a little bit about Ludacris and such. I still have no idea why the Olsen twins are famous, or which is which, but at least I know who they are. You don't have to listen to whatever this month's important rapper does or know who pulled an AK-47 on whom. You don't have to see *I Know What You Did Last Summer* or any Wes Craven movies at all. But you do have to know that Britney lost her virginity to Justin, that Jessica lost hers to Nick, that Christina definitely does not lip-sync, that the second *f* in Fifty Cent is sort of silent. You need to get that Eminem is the only white hip-hop artist who matters, and you have to at least try to understand why twelve-year-old girls are cuckoo-for-Cocoa-Puffs over Jason or Jared or Josh or Justin or whichever one it is on whatever day it is. And you do have to know that they don't think Paul McCartney is Stella's father: They know who the Beatles are, they're not stupid, and they don't deserve to be treated like idiots. You just have to know where it's at, at all times, at least sort of.

Because as bleak as this stuff looks right now, our kids are going to find death-metal music and snuff movies to get into that will be way worse than anything that is produced today. The downward spiral keeps pulling us deeper and deeper into uglier places, rather like a drain sucking used bathwater into the sewer. Outrage only knows how to get more outrageous. People are not nostalgic for no reason (although I must say that baby boomers really must cut it out already). But people also tend to outgrow outrage—at least the worst of it—which is why few rock bands have extensive careers, while Merle Haggard and Frank Sinatra go on forever. Does the menace of Body Count still persist? Does anyone know who Ugly Kid Joe is? And when was the last time you listened to Alice in Chains?

Get my point?

I hope you do. Because one fine day, you will be sitting nervously in your drawing room doing needlepoint, watching Wimbledon with the sound off while some peaceful James Taylor, circa 1974, wafts in the background. At the same time, in a room just down the hall, your pubescent son with dirty hair will be banging his head against the wall to the tune of something very screechy. And at that moment, before you phone the men in white coats to take him away, it might be worth noting that this is just what the kids do and this too shall pass.

Avoid Discomfort

❋

Do I want too much?
Am I going overboard to want that touch?
I shout it out to the night:
Give me what I deserve, 'cause it's my right
LUCINDA WILLIAMS
"Passionate Kisses"

Let's just face it: Woodstock was an event in 1969. Because of a confluence of war, LSD, hippiedom, rain, naked people covered in mud, and traffic backed up on the New York State Thruway for days, Woodstock turned into an event. An *important* event. You didn't even need the musical acts to have a complete Woodstock experience. In fact, you probably could have been in one of those cars trapped in gridlock and still have felt part of this happening.

But that was then. In the wake of the Hell's Angels mess at the Altamont musical gathering that took place not long after Woodstock—a concert captured eerily in the Rolling Stones' documentary *Gimme Shelter*—these outdoor summer extravaganzas should have been put out of business. Perhaps, for a time, they were.

But in recent years, the powers that be have visited upon us Lollapalooza, the Lilith Fair, the Monsters of Rock tour, and many other such multigroup, dank-weather celebrations. I have only one piece of advice: Don't go. Perhaps, at some point in your youth, it was fun to be covered in sweat and carried through a mosh pit and to have warm beer poured all over you—possibly not even by accident. But enough of that. If you are reading this book you are already too old to take part in such unpleasantness. Just give up on ever seeing Sonic Youth play again, unless the venue is someplace nice and spiffy and grownup-friendly.

For that matter, don't go anywhere any time when it is fair to anticipate that you will be out of control of your environment—and said environment will likely be disgusting. Don't get on a sailboat with people you don't know all that well, lest you find yourself stuck in someone else's nautical fantasy. Nothing can be more annoying than a middle-aged man at the boat's helm, spinning its wheel and pointing out where he plays golf or where he hunts seagulls and stuff like that, while you are seasick and unable to escape this little banana republic.

In general, avoid putting your person into any strange situation. I mean, if you are an adventuress and are dying—perhaps quite literally—to skydive into the Himalayas, by all means, be my guest. But as for the rest of us, think long and hard before you get into any scene that involves many compressed and sweaty bodies, mosquitoes, lack of air-conditioning, no running water, and no way out. Avoid tents. If you are told to bring your own sleeping bag, don't go. Do not put yourself that much at the mercy of others. If you didn't go camping when you were a kid, now is not the time to start. You are a big girl and you are entitled to your creature comforts.

Travel Light

*

> . . . and so it goes, and so it goes
> and the book says, "we may be
> through with the past, but the
> past is not through with us."
> PAUL THOMAS ANDERSON
> Magnolia

There is nothing worse than changing planes at an airport and having to schlep a duffel bag full of—who knows?—Armani suits you'll never wear on the beach, eight books that you won't get through in seven days—on a day when for some reason finding an available luggage cart is harder than hailing a taxi in the rain. Compounding the problem is your steely determination to have bought some duty-free Stolichnaya to add to the weight, even though neither you nor anyone you know likes to drink vodka. We all have closets and drawers full of unused fountain pens, unworn rhinestone brooches, untasted loose tea from Harrods, unsprayed bottles of Claude Montana perfume, undisplayed Lalique crystal seashells, and baffling multicolored silk scarves that were purchased at a layover in Frankfurt or Reykjavík. We have all occasionally harbored the belief that saving the tax was more fun than just saving our money.

These behaviors must stop. They cause backaches, headaches, hernias, and foul moods. If you learn to join the ranks of people who just take what they need with them, it will quite literally lighten your load.

It will also make men fall madly in love with you. Every guy who sees you walking through Customs with just a tote bag over your shoulder will think that you are the most amazingly cool chick ever. Because, in the emotional sense, you do not want to be a person who seems to be dragging around a lot of heavy baggage. There is a correlation between people who pack like Rose Dawson in *Titanic* and women who are less than stable while on shore.

While you naturally want to be open, honest, and curious about any person or place or thing that is right in front of you in the present tense, you need not lug the misery of the past into current events and demand that someone who is *not* the father who abused/neglected you years ago be forced to compensate for past wrongs. Honor the statute of limitations, and don't convict the wrong man. Your ancient demons will be more readily deracinated if you cultivate the art of being a person whose needs are met in precise and concise ways.

If It's True Love,
None of the Rules Matter

*

but love is hard to stop
Ted Hughes
"Lovesong"

Hundreds of movies have been made that portray the optimistic—and *realistic*—truth: Love always prevails.

Consider the case of Andie MacDowell and Hugh Grant—a.k.a. Carrie and Charles—in *Four Weddings and a Funeral.* Her marriage to a man three times her age and his aborted nuptials to a woman his friends called "Duckface" did not keep them from getting together in the end. It took some time, and a few unpleasant complications, but they found their way.

And this is not just Hollywood romanticizing reality (never mind that it's a British movie). The honest truth is that when two people connect—I mean *really* connect—it is damn near impossible to keep them apart. In spite of infinite obstacles, ultimately it will become apparent that the powers that be have conspired to bring them together, and no other outcome could be possible. I have friends who are living happily ever after (for now, anyway) with people they'd met when they were married to someone else or living somewhere else or in some way completely unavailable. The long and complicated stories of how they got together—how they kept in touch through marriages and divorces and a tour of duty in Brazil or an assignment in Papua New Guinea—are small and petty and meager compared to the largeness of love.

Which is not to say that you should abandon the etiquette of courtship every time you get that funny feeling that He's The One. For one thing, there will probably be many Ones. Contrary to Plato's *Symposium*, in which all people were once bodily attached to their soul mates to form a human wagon wheel—before being miserably split by the gods as punishment for being too self-satisfied, and forced to roam the world searching for one another's missing halves—

it is not true that only one precious heart belongs with yours. There are many, many people you can and, perhaps, will be happy with in your lifetime; don't let any naysayers tell you otherwise. But when it is absolutely and obviously true love, you can do very little to mess it up or alienate the other person. The situation will simply flow.

I know that there is much talk these days about resuming old-fashioned rules of relationships: of letting the boy approach you first, of waiting for him to call you, of being super-cool—almost chilly—in the beginning. I honestly cannot comment on this, because the people I know in happy couples all got their start in any manner of fashions. In one case, the woman stomped over to the man and said something like, *I am so hot for you and I will die if I can't do you tonight.* In another instance, the man got her number from a friend of a friend after being too shy to talk to her at a cocktail party, and though she had no idea who he was when he called her, she consented to have a drink with him. I am told that people have met at discotheques and orgies, though I have never encountered anyone this has happened to. I know people who have reunited with high school sweethearts, and I know people who have met at work and at poetry readings and at auto dealerships. I know people who have been fixed up by their respective grandmothers. Love is a lawless business—but it does seem that true love tends to take care of its own.

The only boyfriend I have ever been happy with was one who drove me into a multitude of unacceptable behaviors in pursuit of him. In its first year, the relationship was obstacled by the distance between Michigan and Massachusetts, and then in the second year by the lengthier distance between Texas and New York. He had another girlfriend much of the time, and I had several miserable boyfriend situations going on. When we were finally living in the same city, it took a year of seduction, induction, and general harassment to get him to break up with his girlfriend and come back to me.

If it were not true love, I would have seemed like a maniac, and he might have been compelled to call in the authorities. But I was on a righteous mission: I *knew* we belonged together, and the proof was simply in that we *did* get together. Trouble is there is no reliable way to figure out if a person is worth waiting for and struggling with. You won't know until you know, if you see what I mean. This is one of those ends-justifies-the-means situations.

And there is a fine line between love and confusion. If you are sure you hear a voice in your head saying something like, *This time it's the real thing,* it may be intuition—but it may also be the early onset of a mental disorder. That's why it is best to stick to the rules and not throw yourself wholeheartedly into any situation without stepping back from it cautiously at first. If it's love, most of the mechanics of relationship-building will just take care of themselves.

It Doesn't Matter When You Sleep with Someone for the First Time, But You Have to Really Be Ready

*

We all know that no matter how we try to separate sex from love, in real life it doesn't work that way. You say to yourself, as you take some new stranger home with you on some night that involves a little too much tequila, *I am not in love with this person; I am not even quite sure of his name; I just think he is hotter than August and I wanna fuck him.* You pretend that you are Samantha on *Sex and the City*. You tell yourself that in spite of his long beautiful blond hair that reminds you of Gregg Allman's (I'm afraid I'm dating myself a bit here) or his extremely cheeky smile that makes you forget everything else you ever knew, you know that he is just not right for you. He does not speak the Queen's English, or perhaps he does not even speak English at all. Or his combined SAT scores are in the three digits, and he thinks that Lord Byron is the name of a rock star (sort of true). There are a million reasons you can find to convince yourself that some guy is twenty feet beneath you, nothing more than a toy, useful only for his immediate stud purposes. So, seeing as he is completely inappropriate for a smart, educated girl like you who read *Middlemarch* all the way through and wears real pearls and Chanel No. 5, you will be certain that you can take him home for a wild night, fuck him through the roof, and when it's all over, you might just ask him what his name is.

This is, after all, something that men seem to do with the greatest of ease. And in this postfeminist world, you ought to be able to do it too.

You think you can manage that.

And maybe you can.

But the mind will play tricks on you. Personally,

over the years there have been so many men who were all wrong for me, who I *knew* I didn't belong with and I knew it so well that I thought it was safe to sleep with them, that it wouldn't mean a thing—and then the next morning I'm naming our children, all six of them, and wondering what snobby, snotty notions make me think that a high school dropout who works as a gardener is beneath me. I try to think of him as a *botanist*. Meanwhile, said gardener is sound asleep or pretending to be, hoping I'll be gone by the time he wakes up. (And this is in *my* home.)

Point is, sex is such a loaded activity that people wish someone would set a rule about when it's okay to do it—and when it's not. Unfortunately, it's impossible to say whether it should be on the first date or the fortieth; in fact, it makes no difference.

But you do have to know *why* you're doing whatever it is that you're doing, because it changes everything; the whole nature of the relationship is transformed by the act of sex. Often women become more needy and insecure after it's happened, there's no getting around that. And I personally would rather be needy and insecure with someone I've been hanging out with for a while—but that's just me. Don't make the mistake of believing that if a savage night of hot sex makes you wake up with the urge to go shopping for wallpaper, the guy you're with will feel the same. Likewise, if you *know* that you are going to rise in the morning with some such domestic compulsion, consider if it would not be wiser to wait awhile.

Always Keep Your Mind on How You Feel, Not on How He Feels

*

If I am what I am because I am what I am,
and if you are what you are because you are what you are,
then I am what I am and you are what you are.
But if I am what I am because you are what you are,
and you are what you are because I am what I am,
then I am not what I am and you are not what you are.

YASMINA REZA

ART

If you are like me—and probably like most of us—you wander self-consciously through life, wondering what other people are thinking about you, frightened that they are judging you. Since, most likely, all these other people are walking around with the same self-conscious thoughts, you need not worry what they think about you, because they probably don't. The sooner you realize this, the easier it will be for you to glide through life, unscathed and unconcerned.

This preoccupation with what other people think is particularly nefarious when it involves a man you are into. In the beginning of a relationship, you are always walking around with a daisy, plucking at its petals, wondering if he loves you or loves you not. In the meanwhile, you may very easily lose sight of how *you* feel about him. And you sit around with your friends and analyze every little move—as if.

Truth is, studying tea leaves, throwing the *I Ching,* reading the Tarot, or talking to a psychic might give you some insight into what is going on—but only into what is going on with *you.* Barring paranormal powers, you really cannot possibly ascertain what he thinks and feels. If he calls and wants to spend time with you, these are pretty good indications that he is at least falling in *like* with you, but beyond that, things can go any which way, and you probably just have to wait and see. More will be revealed.

Meanwhile, every time you find yourself wondering how *he* feels about you, if *he* likes you, if *he* loves you, if *he* wants you desperately, try instead to start asking yourself how *you* feel about him. Because that's what really counts, that's all you can possibly know, and that's really what you need to be figuring out. A lot of times, your wondering about his emotions may in fact reflect your own ambivalence: maybe *you* don't adore him so damn much; maybe you just *want* to want him—which is silly. So often we are so eager to be in love and happy and all that stuff that we forget to keep track of what we really think of any one particular guy. Men seem less likely to fall into this trap.

For an assortment of biological and sociological reasons—most of which are just plain not fair—men are rarely so eager to get into a relationship that they are willing to overlook some lady's appalling table manners, her affected British accent, and the potently ugly shade of orange eye shadow that she wears in broad daylight. Women, on the other hand, often seem prepared to believe that Hitler was just an animal-loving vegetarian and ignore the rest. This is a problem. This is how we find our way into relationships that don't work out, but that leave us obsessively self-loathing, wondering, *Why didn't he like me?* Somehow, we forget that he has all the charisma of Al Gore, that he has all the sex appeal of Dick Cheney, that he sweats like Albert Brooks, that he dances like a white man, and that he loves the Carpenters with complete sincerity.

You will, in other words, be obsessed with a man who, by all rights, you should not even like.

It is time to stop the insanity. Keep track of your thoughts about the latest Lothario, and don't just fall for any old guy who is giving you a hard time on that particular week. Before you waste a year with a waste of time, check out your own opinion of the guy. In all the time you invest in some loser, you could probably have met twenty people who would make you pleased as punch and ready to kick up your heels and jitter-bug. Once again, you will have to trust me on this one. As soon as you start to focus on and honor your own heart, much else will fall into place.

Don't Try to be Friends
with Your Exes

*

I can't survive on what you send
Every time you need a friend
BILLY BRAGG
"A New England"

Don't pretend. Don't kid yourself. You *know* that you are just waiting for him to come back, or he is just waiting for you to give up and give in—neither of you really wants to be friends, because that's not how it works. Someone who is hurting you—which is usually what goes on when people break up—is by definition *not* your friend. If someone was important to you and you want to keep in touch in a general way and have coffee and reminisce once every couple of years to mark the milestone that this relationship was, that's fine; go ahead and meet at Dunkin' Donuts, or send a Christmas card, or accept a collect call now and again.

But the myth of friendship with a former lover— with rare exceptions—is one of the sexual revolution's most glaring and least noticed bits of chicanery. Whether you've been dumped or done the dumping, why would you want to make repeated visits to the site of such an emotional car wreck? What is the point of such torture? If you need a friend, go to the animal shelter and adopt one. But don't mistake "friendship" for friendship.

Having stridently stated my position, I must retreat slightly and offer a small reprieve. But do beware: *This proviso applies only to the period immediately following a messy breakup.* Because, in all fairness, few of us can live up to this lofty standard right away, since losing a lover is, of course, also the loss of a dear friend and constant companion. After the initial split, you are allowed a grace period—don't let this last for more than a month or two, depending on how long you were in the couple and how maladjusted the rift leaves you—during which there may be some back and forth, some talk of reuniting, and, of course, some nights engaging in the carnal misery of post-relationship sex.

Girls, trust me on this one: The worst kind of sex is the type you have with someone you've just broken up with, because it gives false hope and creates much confusion the morning after about *what it means* and *what to do*. Usually one or the other of you—and in my experience, it is always he—has to go to work or has a tennis match scheduled, which means you will be left with that obsessive, mixed-up feeling all day. The only reason this kind of carrying-on is acceptable is simply that it will wear you down so thoroughly that you will eventually fall on your hands and knees and pray for relief from this sick situation, and suddenly enough will be enough.

You will realize, with great serenity, that all this headless-hen activity has mostly diverted your energy from the joyous task of getting on with your life.

Be Righteously Indignant

✳

And when she burns you again
And your phone doesn't ring
Baby it's me

MARY CHAPIN CARPENTER
"Never Had It So Bad"

B ut use in moderation.

Don't be Paula Jones, don't mistake a trivial
bit of trouble for a big fucking deal. Which is not to
say that Ms. Jones did not have a right to be all hot
and bothered about the way Bill Clinton allegedly
treated her in a hotel hospitality suite some many
years ago. It's just that her lawsuit pretty much defines
what people mean when they say, *You don't have to make*
a federal case out of it. The woman has since been mar-

ried and had children; her career—or, I should say, her employment—was in no way jeopardized by this ten-minute encounter, however unpleasant. And if it really bothered her so much, she should have done something about it at the time, not later on, when he's president and the whole situation is more juicy. Everyone, including the biggest asshole on earth, deserves due process. Paula Jones would have received much more sympathy from many feminists—myself included—had she handled her complaint in a timely fashion.

Storing up your righteous indignation for eventual tactical use is not playing fair, girls. I know that a buildup of anger can become a seething and brutal weapon just waiting to be brandished at the foes that be. But learn to fight like a lady. A good duel has always been a gentleman's sport, and therefore a favored form of execution; we of the fairer sex should take a lesson from that example. Unless you are going to join up in some class action suit brought by a collective of victims years down the road, best to neatly face and tidy up life's infractions and infringements in their right time and place, trying as hard as you can to be as straightforward and absolute as a gunshot. After you have settled the score—or just plain old decided that it is not worth it—it is best to walk on, leaving life's injustices and inequities behind you.

You have got to be doubly strict about your conduct on the more personal front. Because a long time after you have forgotten about what or who it was that made you so mad, you will remember if you did or didn't comport yourself with dignity—and if it's the former, it will stay with you like a trophy on the mantel. On the other hand, if you throw a tantrum that involves name-calling, dish-throwing, book-burning, waking up the neighbors, generally disturbing the peace, chasing someone down the street with a machete—if the matter ends with one or both of you spending the night in jail, this is just not good.

Here are some simple clues about how to get righteously indignant with grace. The most important rule is don't get third parties involved, don't ask friends and go-betweens to transmit messages—this will do nothing except make the other person feel manipulated and make you feel like you're back in sixth grade. When a man has hurt your feelings, let him know just how bad he's made you feel—and stand by it. If you tell someone to fuck off and die, mean it—which is to say, don't expect him to come crawling back; don't bluff if you're not prepared to have it called. That's a really important one, because many a foolish young woman has dumped her boyfriend as a power play, expecting him to prostrate himself before her feet and beg for forgiveness, only to find that he's left so quickly there are skid marks on her anteroom floor, and within two weeks he is seen around town with some very annoying, statuesque French girl who smokes Gauloises and calls herself Zaza.

Clearly, this is not the result you hoped for.

Righteous indignation is a liberating, invigorating emotion that you can only really feel when you are certain that you are right, when you know that you have been wronged. It does not visit itself upon you very often, so savor it, bury yourself in it, wear its warmth like a shearling coat. Tell your ex-boyfriend bluntly to his face that you are baffled as to how such a lousy lay could have sundered your heart so completely. But think long and hard before you do it. If you don't really mean it, you will come across as a desperate, raving lunatic, and not as a woman he once loved—and possibly still loves: a woman who is now serenely and resolutely walking out of his door.

The Only Way to Get One Person Off Your Mind Is to Get Another One on Your Body

*

Of course, this action could easily backfire, so it is only recommended when you really know what you are doing.

This is a situation where ex-boyfriends in good standing can be helpful. But they have to be men you have truly lost interest in. Years ago. You have to pick a man whom you are vaguely and glancingly in touch with (i.e., the one you occasionally see at Dunkin'

Donuts), someone you respect enough that his attentions can still make your heart flutter and your body shiver just a little bit—but not too much. Not enough that you will find yourself—heaven forfend!—wanting to get back together with him the next day. Because if you sleep with one man to get *un*obsessed with another man, the last thing you want is two men who give you paroxysms of agony, and not much else.

Your emotional life, in the aftermath of a breakup, will be sufficiently messy that you should only do comforting and nourishing things with yourself. This is a good time for facials and massages, but *absolutely no haircuts:* Women in the throes of heartbreak have been known to enter a salon with long, lovely locks— and to exit it looking like Johnny Rotten, circa 1978. Harm reduction should be your priority when your heart aches like it's more than just a vital organ, so be careful what you do.

In a desperate desire to get away from the horror of your own head, it is perfectly understandable that you will hitch your wagon to some very unfortunate characters and situations. If there is some guy out there who can be of any aid to you in your delicate condition, by all means use him as a resource, exhaust his energy until he has completely sapped yours.

Fuck your brains out in the bed you used to share with your boyfriend, and think *ha ha ha ha ha* the whole time.

But know thyself—and, for that matter, kid thyself not. If you feel even sort of like you are about to be inhaled into a situation that might go from bad to weird, do refrain.

Do Nothing

✳

With a certain amount of introspection, triggered by age,
plain old maturity, you find that it doesn't hurt so bad not
to be in the eye of the hurricane.

BETTE MIDLER

This is a really hard one. It is hard because it is about cultivating a deep passivity in your emotional life—a tender calm that would probably be very detrimental to other aspects of your existence. So don't start thinking that doing nothing is about whiling away the hours sitting on your settee and eating bonbons when you should be at work trying to change the world in whatever little way you can. Doing nothing is not the same as being a lazy, useless bum.

Doing nothing is the opposite of, say, shagging

some guy so that you can stop thinking about some other guy. Or calling your recent ex-boyfriend in a state of desperation to tell him that you cannot live without him when, by virtue of the fact that you are still breathing without the least bit of medical intervention, this is simply not true: you *can* live without him, you *have* lived without him, and you *will* continue to live without him.

Doing nothing is about making a conscious decision to not accelerate the drama. It is about refusing to succumb to the pull of escapism, even though it is so much more appealing than the reality of life at the moment. Doing nothing means not drinking a whole flask of cognac, and it means not spending the next day vomiting and lying in bed with the kind of headache that doesn't go away no matter how you position yourself or your pillow. It means not booking a flight to Morocco—because good sources have reported that there is no such thing as pain in Marrakech—when you know you have neither the money nor the time to make this excursion. It means not calling various people in your life to threaten suicide when you know perfectly well that's not what's going to happen.

Doing nothing means calmly asking for help

when you need it, and taking what good you can receive from people who care about you, even though, in hard times, it will probably never feel like enough.

Doing nothing is opting for the sweetness of stillness. It is about just sitting with your loneliness, making some effort to accept how bad you feel, not resorting to the kind of behavior that you know deep down inside is just not a good idea. It is about taking long, contemplative walks through Central Park, meeting girlfriends for tea and reading silly self-help books until you know every pop psychologist's theory about women and fear of abandonment and lack of object constancy and inability to use anger in constructive ways. It means checking out the horoscopes in Elle and Vogue and Marie Claire, and comparing them for common and inconsistent predictions. It is about doing no more than these nice, quiet things that you are sure will not hurt you. It is about not pursuing histrionics and hysteria, it is about knowing that only time and peace of mind will make things better.

What it comes down to is this: Instead of fighting with that which you cannot control, you might as well just see it through. If you were skiing and suddenly confronted by an avalanche, you would not argue with the snow and demand that it sort itself out and stop attacking you; you would do the best you could to get the hell out of the way.

And doing nothing is not just something you must try in the case of a broken heart. It is the operative rule with office altercations, screaming fights with your mother, and unpleasant tiffs with friends and lovers. If you try to force a resolution to some situation that needs only to be left alone to diffuse, you are only going to worry a wound. Very often the solution has nothing to do with the problem. Going bicycling or making a trip to see the pandas at the zoo is more likely to solve your little misunderstandings than more hours of babble and battle. In a perfect example of stuffy, sensible, and unmistakably British wisdom, Dame Rose Macauley once noted that "It is a common delusion that you can make things better by talking about them."

In all these situations, if you just step back and go about your workaday life, the drama will take care of itself. In fact, it will usually completely burn up in its own angry pyre, because as much as you don't like having mishaps with people in your life, they too don't much like having them with you. So don't pick up the phone so that you can add in just one *last* last word. Don't go running through the streets late at night, and ring your boyfriend's doorbell with a floral peace offering because you cannot bear the thought that he might maybe never speak to you again. All this activity is simply unnecessary, annoyingly tiresome, and cloyingly manipulative.

I know they say that couples should not go to sleep angry, but in the big, messy mishmash of lovers' fights, sometimes you can't avoid going to bed angry; the idea is not to go to sleep angrier. Much as you might feel inclined to dissect the innards of your quarrels, so long as they are not habitual, it is not a bad idea to just leave things be.

I feel it is only right for me to confess here that learning to do nothing has pretty much saved my life. I feel a bit hypocritical telling anyone not to get drunk and drugged and disorderly, or not to go too far in whatever which way, because, God knows, at times that has been the story of my life. But it was exhausting and taxing beyond what I or the people around me could live with, and eventually enough became enough. You are entitled to your years of bad scenes and rotten hangovers, but when you get to be a bit older—say, over thirty—and you are ready to surrender craziness as a lifestyle choice, you should learn how to do nothing. By learning to bury my impetuous desire to act out when I have *no idea* what might be the next right thing to do, I have found that in the times that I could have spent making matters worse, I have actually managed to finish the Sunday *New York Times* crossword puzzle. Or I have gone to see a Preston Sturges double feature. Or I have sat through *Barry Lyndon* in its entirety. Or I have learned the difference between peppermint and spearmint.

In the time I have wasted making matters worse, I could have easily raised six children. Without a father. Without even a nanny.

So just believe me: Don't do something about whatever crazy feelings are boxing in your head until you have first tried to just do nothing. You will be amazed to discover that feelings are not facts, and feelings can be trusted to go away. They always do. I promise. And when they leave—probably with great alacrity if you have avoided doing anything to fuck things up further—you will feel much, much better.

When All Else Fails, Talk to God

*

> For when you need me I will do
> What your own mother didn't do
> Which is to mother you
> SINÉAD O'CONNOR
> "This Is to Mother You"

Believe it or not, conversations with the Omnipotent will actually do a lot to make you feel better, even if you do not particularly believe in God. Maybe even *especially* if you don't believe in God. Because if you have no faith, prayer will actually do a lot to get you to that place where you believe in *something*. And it's good to believe in something. If you don't have some sense that there is a force out there that has the run of things, if you feel utterly at the mercy of yourself and the whims of the world, there is a good chance that you will go through much of life feeling extremely depressed and desolate. This is why people join cults and end up dying from cyanide-laced Kool-Aid in a petty dictatorship in South America, and this is why Richard Gere hangs out with the Dalai Lama.

Everyone needs something to hold on to.

So it might not be a bad idea to cultivate a relationship with a kind, benevolent God, one whom you believe is on your side. Much as I want to deprecate Madonna's adoption of Kabbalah and Courtney Love's immersion in Kundalini yoga, I must admit that they seem like happier and calmer people as a result of this activity. This does not mean that you have to go to church, synagogue, or a mosque—but, hey, whatever gets you through the night. It certainly does not mean you have to read *The Celestine Prophecy* or any of the extensive oeuvre of Deepak Chopra—in fact, I would avoid that stuff for dear life.

You just have to try really hard to find within yourself the capacity for hope, grace, and joy, for the ecstatic possibilities that you can only have if you embrace the idea of some larger plan that makes the trifling daily insults and indignities seem small, which they are. Besides, if you talk to God about what you want from life and how shitty you feel about this or that, you will probably find that you feel better. I could not tell you why, but it works for me, and I am a serious doubter.

I first became interested in developing a repertoire of godly appeals after reading an article several years ago in *Newsweek* about the practical efficacy of prayer. It seems that a study was done using the immediate kin of people suffering from cancer or other terminal—though possibly curable—illnesses. One group of the people in the study prayed each day for the souls of their beloveds, and the other group did not. As things worked out, the patients who were prayed for had a monumentally higher rate of recovery than the ones who just got visits and flower arrangements.

Perhaps even more interesting is that the group of worshippers was divided in two—one half asked for specific things (e.g., restoring their loved ones to health), while the other group just meditatively reached out to God or whatever they believed in, and said simply, "Thy will be done." The relatives of those in the latter group fared better than the ones in the former. Which is to say, simple trust in the world's wish to return to balance after imposing instability and pain, simple belief that the will of God is to care for you and yours—faith alone will see you through.

Another nice thing about supplicating only to have God's will carried out as it is intended for you—which at first seems kind of ridiculous, since if He is all-powerful, that's what's going to happen anyway—is that it allows you to ask that the universe do right by you even when you yourself have no idea what "right" is. And what is "right" usually turns out to be what happens when you just get out of your own way, when you don't thwart all possibility of happiness by trying to manipulate events that you cannot—and should not—control. The participants in *Newsweek*'s study were in a situation that they most probably knew they had little hold on; in a situation like that, it is easy to give prayer a chance, since nothing else is left.

Interestingly, it seems not to have mattered whether these people were faithful or religious to begin with—prayer did not discriminate between those who identified themselves as believers and those who did not. Whether praying helped because God really does exist and care, or if it is useful simply because it made the patients in question feel more cared for and more in touch with the possibility of their own spiritual redemption, is not for me to say. All I know is that somehow prayer works.

Sooner or later, all paths lead to God.

Think Productively

✳

*I guess I could be pretty pissed off about what happened
to me, but it's hard to stay mad, when there's so much
beauty in the world. Sometimes I feel like I'm seeing it all
at once, and it's just too much, my heart fills up like a
balloon that's about to burst. And then I remember to
relax, and stop trying to hold on to it, and then it flows
through me like rain and I can't feel anything but
gratitude for every single moment of my stupid little life.*

ALAN BALL
American Beauty

I must grudgingly admit that I do believe in the
power of positive thinking, if only because the em-
pirical evidence is in its favor. I could not possibly
keep a straight face while engaging in daily affirma-

tions or meditations or mantras (whatever they are), but I recognize the success of The Little Engine That Could. It seems pretty apparent that you have to be sure that you are worthy or deserving of whatever it is you want before you get it. For instance, if you think—as I have been known to do—something like, *I am so horrible, I am completely unlovable, what man will ever want me?*, there is a pretty good chance that you will see that prediction through. Sadly, self-fulfilling prophecies are a documented fact. So, according to experts and happy people everywhere—those who know—you are only as fortunate as your expectations. Apparently, it's not that you have to see it to believe it; on the contrary, you have to *believe* it to see it.

It goes without saying that your mind will wander where it may: to thoughts of millennial doom, to images of a body with every inch of skin coated in cellulite, to the horror of contemplating another stint as a bridesmaid in another hot-pink puffy-shouldered dress that the bride will insist you can later have tailored into cocktail garb, to a certainty that you will not be accepted to the university of your choice, and that you will never rise beyond an entry-level position in your career. In other words, you will convince yourself that all the variables in your life will never align harmonically all at once, and you will always be malcontent and pathetic.

Now, let's face it: Any or all the aforementioned unpleasantries are distinctly possible. But dwelling on it will clearly only make the possible into the probable. Also, all your worry about the future—or your regret over the past—will wreak havoc on the present. (I once heard somebody say that if you have one leg in the past and another in the future, you are pissing on the here and now.) While systematically going through each particular cause of anxiety might allay your fears for a little while, the truth is that the only way to really relieve your weary and hyperactive mind is to simply stop. *Just stop it!* STOP IT! Just like that. Banish these thoughts from your brain, treat them like marauding intruders at your doorway: *Don't let them in.* They are as spiritually and emotionally contaminating as any virus is physically debilitating. So protect yourself; don't indulge.

And this prescription holds true for anything in your life. Perhaps you cannot help feeling that you are, say, a pathetic hopeless case of some sort, that one day you will be murdered by a madman whom you picked up at a bar late one night, that pieces of your body will be crammed into rubbish bins all over town, and no one will even notice that you are dead until the rent is due. Although even hypnosis, medication, and years of therapy might not be able to expel this nagging, insidious fear from your subconscious, you can avoid adding credence to it on a conscious level by refusing to engage with this silly idea. It is, quite simply, absurd. And you just have to make it a full-time preoccupation to stop being preoccupied by your negative self-assessment. Because, even if you are among the fewer than one percent of people who will live this fate, you have to pretend it is not so. And if you pretend for long enough, you will soon be convinced. Oh yes, you will.

And things will change. Even if that miserable life and death once *was* your destiny, you might actually change the outcome by your newfound faith in yourself. Think of it this way: If you shift the projectile that is your life by only one degree, it will not look so different at first. But if the line protruding from that slightly different angle is allowed to run on for months and years, it will soon be at a completely different place from the starting point. The result will be wholly unimaginably altered, just as the slightly different increments of time change the various dénouements in the German movie *Run Lola Run*. If you even modify your assumptions about yourself in the *smallest* way—say, start believing that you *will* pick up a madman in a bar one night, and he *will* murder you, but you will be sorely missed by masses of people—it will reroute the course of your life, bit by bit, until it is completely different.

It is useless to always assume you are one of those people stuck in life with the odds stacked against you. And while you may believe that your lowly estimation of yourself is an indication of your modest nature and lack of pride, you are wrong. In fact, believing that your life will be a dreadful disaster is an extremely self-centered and self-involved view of the world, because it assumes that you are like no one else on earth. Whether you think you are better or worse off than everybody else does not make much difference: in either case you have separated yourself and your life from the rules that govern the rest of humanity. Sometimes it may feel like that is the case, but it's not. I mean, what makes *you* so uniquely cursed? What about *you* is so gruesomely hideous that you will never find the happiness that you crave?

If most people manage to get married, have children, stay employed, pay taxes, and whatever else, then there is no reason to believe that all these matters will fail to fall into place for you at their rightful time. Now, if you have big, bold dreams—you long to be the next Madame Curie, you want to paint like Georgia O'Keeffe or write like Emily Brontë—you probably will need a touch of genius and a lot of study and practice to get it right. But most of us have far simpler, purer—and more beautiful—wishes and wants. For most of us, it is enough to just be glad to be alive. And that's a lot.

Enjoy Your Single Years

✳

Je ne regrette rien
EDITH PIAF

Do not view the years between college and marriage—and I hope we are talking *years* and not months, or heaven forbid, days—as one long preamble to real life. Worse still, do not view the years between kindergarten and marriage, between your first Oasis concert and marriage, between losing your virginity and marriage—frankly, between any convenient milestone and the day of your nuptial vows—as life in abeyance. Do not think that the whole point of being single is getting married; men don't think this way, and neither should you. Your single years, in and of themselves, are extremely important, not to be traded for the Taj Mahal or the Hope diamond or anything—and do not let your grandmother tell you otherwise.

And there are, unfortunately, many people besides your grandmother who will tell you otherwise, and they should be promptly put out of their misery with the nearest available weapon. Because these people exist on this planet for the sole purpose of upsetting and confusing you and anyone else with common sense: By playing upon your fears, they can be surprisingly convincing. These people are evil. In fact, all cahoots of culture that suggest to young women that they ought to rush to the altar while their flesh is still tender and their skin is still taut are doing these girls a great disservice.

Because if you marry too young, you will always wonder. Wonder about the boyfriends you will never have—unless you take up with them illicitly—and about the singular solo personality that you will never develop, and about the trashy, flashy outfits that you will never get to wear—at least not outside your own bedroom—because you are a nice married lady, you are a very good girl. You will wonder about everything. Even if you are happy with your husband and think he is the greatest thing since Cool Whip, you will wonder what you are missing.

Because in a world that encourages interpersonal curiosity, you are not going to be exempt from such a typical tendency. This is not the nineteenth century. People are not spending large parts of their lives in sanatoria, suffering from consumption in a Thomas Mann vision of romantic pallor. People no longer die young and pretty of lung conditions and fatigue. By the time we are little old ladies, all of us will be living to age two hundred, settled in condominium colonies on the moon, and living on a steady diet of Ovaltine and Tang. Given this situation, it seems like a good idea to choose wisely when seeking out the man with whom you want to spend a gravity-free old age. These days, until death do you part is a *very* long time, and despite the prevalence of divorce, I do believe that all of us still wish to wed only once. It is not a bad idea to grow into yourself just a wee bit before you try to blend in with someone else.

Now, I know that after sixteen boyfriends and sixty one-night stands, you start to wonder when— or if—it will ever end. But you must endure; you must relish the instability to the absolute best of your ability; don't ask why, just believe me: *you must.* Somewhere, in the pile of debris that you will accumulate for the rest of your life, is a point to every misbegotten rendezvous, every bad sexual encounter where some guy mistook your clitoris for an elevator button and you faked an orgasm just to make it end; someday, I promise, you will be able to plot these points on a spreadsheet, and the sensible curve that is your life will become clear, inevitable—you will see all these events for *just what they were,* and you will know that it could not have happened any other way.

But sometimes, after one too many crusty, drymouthed Sunday mornings with a bad headache and a blunted memory, you may start to wish that you had been betrothed at birth to the boy next door. You may start to think that you ought to shack up with the next truck driver who gives you a double take. It may start to seem like every man you meet is your last chance, the only person who knows the way to the one still-open shelter on the eve of a nuclear war. It may start to seem like every guy you come across— the butcher, the courier, the fellow you sit opposite every morning on the subway, your fifteen-year-old brother's school friend—is the only person left that you haven't *already* met, that you have not *already* spent a bad, boring night with. But this isn't true. You are never too old, jaded, wasted, and used by the world to feel young, dreamy, surprised, and amazed by life and love once again. You should not give up five minutes before the miracle is about to happen.

And besides: *You must take your chances.* You must even take your chances that you will never find someone to marry. This won't happen, by the way, but you are better off living with that possibility than hiding from life. Because it's fun to be single and to live in a house or apartment that belongs to you and only you, that is decorated with your favorite bric-a-brac from some flea market, and with Oriental rugs that you carried back from Turkey yourself. And it's fun to go to Turkey yourself—or to Tasmania or Ibiza or Montana or Montenegro. It's fun to do almost everything by yourself: to have high tea at the Plaza in the late afternoon, to read a magazine and eat breakfast early in the morning. It's fun to walk through Greenwich Village alone, to shop at the flea market alone, to wander through New Orleans alone, to look down into the miserable polluted waters of Lake Michigan alone, to visit the Andy Warhol Museum in Pittsburgh alone, to drive along the Pacific Coast Highway alone, to see the Dictators play in some dive on New Year's Eve alone. Really.

It would not, of course, be much amusement to do *all* these things by yourself *all the time,* which is why even single girls are allowed to have friends and paramours and escorts for nights at the theater. Certainly, I think it is extremely ill advised to either have children alone or climb Mount Everest on your own—which is why at least the latter is prohibited by Nepalese law. But you—like every human being on this planet, all of us who must suffer the fate of being born alone and finally dying alone—must cultivate the ability to enjoy your own company. To enjoy it thoroughly. If you cannot sit still long enough to read a book by yourself while sipping cappuccino at some charming little cul-de-sac café, or if you think attending a movie *à une* is one of those activities that you'll just leave to the artsy girls in black berets who swagger when they walk, you have serious problems on your hands. Until you overcome this silly inability to be alone in these perfectly appropriate ways, you should recognize that you are also completely unsuitable for the married life of togetherness. You are not, for that matter, suitable for much of anything, and should probably force yourself to take up some of these solo activities several times a week until they become as comfortable to you as a crowd of friends.

Basically, what I am trying to say here is: Don't even think of getting married until you are quite certain that you've outgrown your little-girl days of being a whiny, needy pain in the ass. Until you have become the fascinating, fabulous person that *you* would want to spend the rest of *your* life with, don't impose your imprecise and immature existence on anybody else.

And remember, as I keep repeating, the women's movement did not come along to ruin our lives and deprive us of happy homes. It happened because women wanted and needed time to come into their own alone. Even with all the miserable stuff you will have to put up with as a single woman—the heartaches and bad jobs and damp, dark one-room efficiencies in bad neighborhoods—it is worth the adventure, worth the trouble. And all those youthful indiscretions—what would life be without them? Do not accept anyone else's standards or any conventional wisdom about activities you will likely live to regret: It almost goes without saying that if you are endowed with common sense, you will one day think you were slightly mad for posing nude in *Playboy*, for stripping your way through college, or for refusing Prince Charles' hand in marriage. But so what? That's for you to figure out. You must relish your own idiocy, because at times it will seem like it's the only thing you have.

And very rarely has anyone's life actually been ruined by the stupid things they have done when they were young and dopey (Princess Diana—who *did* marry Prince Charles—may be the glaring exception). Take Vanessa Williams, for example: She is the only Miss America whose entertainment career did not end with a tiara on her head and a sash across her body—or by doing orange juice advertisements, or by marrying the host of a game show. Of course, Ms. Williams was dethroned when some sapphic photographs taken when she was nineteen years old and having a swinging time surfaced in *Penthouse* magazine. But hardly anyone can any longer remember that exhibit—or her rather more embarrassing days as a beauty pageant queen—because her life went on. And I have no doubt that Vanessa Williams' public persona evolved in an interesting fashion because she actually did know how to really live it up in private—and she knew how to simply get up and get on with it. And really, *that* is the secret to this whole business of life: You must cultivate the dignity to walk away before they make you run. (Even Richard Nixon was possessed of this small personal asset.)

People who behave in a silly way do not end up with limited lives of no substance—to the contrary: The miserable fate of having nothing ever happen to you is reserved for those who never do anything. So do dumb things and do them with impunity. Spend your nights crying on the bathroom floor, and your icky, incandescent early mornings searching for the last traces of cocaine on the white tile. Sleep with married members of Congress. Male and female. Look back laughingly on youthful folly.

Just so long as you outgrow it. The worst is doing these things when you are not young enough to toss them off with any semblance of grace, the worst is to end up drunk, dead, over a guardrail and up a tree, when you are fifty-two and already way too old to be driving around in that sporty red convertible that you bought yourself as a half-century birthday present—to the baffled humiliation of your already estranged and alienated teenage children. I like to call that sort of behavior approaching middle age from the wrong end, and that is the only thing you really need to be afraid of.

Meanwhile, learn a lesson from Rickie Lee Jones, who was once one of the great youthful disaster areas, particularly in her days as half of a couple with Tom Waits, when they were just a pair of junkies heading for the junkyard. Somehow Ms. Jones made a remarkable recovery into the world of sanity—by the way, no need to make as many mistakes as she did in order to become a grown-up, but it need not necessarily be the end of the world—and she finally settled down and had a child. When daughter Charlotte was born, Ms. Jones wrote her a song called "The Horses," full of promises of safe shelter from life's vicissitudes and lots of wild pony rides along the way. She makes motherhood sound like much more fun than it ever was for my mom. The song ends with the only words you must hope to be able someday to say to your offspring: "And when I was young, oh I was a wild, wild one."

But Do Settle Down

❋

The love you take
Is equal to the love you make
JOHN LENNON AND
PAUL MCCARTNEY
"The End"

Because having a family is a happy thing.

After you have swung from the best Waterford crystal chandeliers that someone else's money can buy; after you have been through any of the combined humiliations of being duped and dumped for your much-less-attractive best friend or canned for your much-more-inferior rival; after you have traveled through the former Soviet Union with nothing but a weak high school knowledge of French to get you between youth hostels; after—and this is the *real* challenge—you have, *just once,* enjoyed a New Year's Eve when you didn't have a boyfriend and you were not so drunk or high or wired that you were vomiting out the window of some stranger's crowded and congested, noisy and noisome party—when you were able to just spend a relatively quiet night with a few truly dear friends; after you have done those things, so that somewhere between satiation and saturation you have even achieved the occasional state of grace, then you are ready to call it quits. Enough is enough. You have successfully run the gauntlet of single life, and now it is time to collect your bag of party favors, and move on. You've been single long enough. You don't want your life to go into reruns, so stop the syndication deal before it starts. Enough. It's time to settle down. So find some good man and just do it.

Just like that.

And don't worry: When you are good and ready— *good* and *ready* being operative words here—the right man will just show up. He just will. Unplanned but entirely expected, like a dandelion growing on the front lawn, there he will be. You won't need a book like *The Rules* or *Getting the Love You Deserve* or anything like that, because he will just sort of show up. All of your dreams and schemes, and in the end, there he will be, somebody else and somewhere else and something else entirely. *Life is what happens while you're busy making other plans.* If you get nothing else out of reading this book, I hope it will be that when you take care of yourself and tend to your garden like Voltaire instructed us all to do, life will do its part to take care of you. In fact, all I or anyone else can possibly offer is some comfort until you arrive at this tranquil place—a place that, with or without anybody's words of wisdom, you will eventually get to because the flow of existence will row you there. Whether you choose to go kicking and screaming or opt to make things as easy as possible for yourself are the only variables that there are.

(As one who has made things as difficult as possible for herself all the way through, far be it from me to counsel others to take the duller, softer route.)

And the truth is, when you are ready to settle in and settle down, the hard part will be *avoiding* your life-partner, the challenge will be the millions of tricks that you will treat yourself to in an effort to thwart this inevitability, to stop true happiness as it greets you everywhere you look. The temptation to run from that which you have always hoped, prayed, and wished for—particularly if happiness has always

been a stranger to you—may well be your predomi-
nant impulse in the face of true love. But you are just
going to have to get a grip. Don't postpone, deny, or
derail joy. Because at a certain point, you actually will
start to become sufficiently fucked up that you actually *can* get in the way of life's inevitable, happy flow,
you actually *can* start doing the kinds of things that
will mess you up for good, and you will turn into one
of those lonely miserable people who cannot have
relationships and who starts creeping deeper and
deeper into middle age, less able to love and more
likely to live and die alone. I say this not to make you
panic—you have plenty of years and chances to go
before you will reach this point—but if you have
played out your days as a single girl, and a good person comes along offering you his heart and all you do
is skewer it to bits, you are going to start becoming
an *actually troubled person*, as opposed to just an evolv-
ing woman who is figuring things out. You are going
to start getting what you deserve, and it will not be
pretty or cute or charming at all.

And there is just no need for this.

While the occasional Isaac Newton among us is
going to be satisfied by a life under the apple tree
without any of the Andrews Sisters or anyone else for

company, for most of us the abstract beauty of the world's offerings will mean nothing at all with no one to share them with. The corniness of purple-pink sunsets and the starkness of starry nights and the pristine purity of white, white snow and the hallucinatory pleasure of red, red wine are lonelier than a Roy Orbison song when you are all alone. You've got to give it time and give yourself time and do all the other things I told you to do first, to be ready for the real big love that life has planned for you, but sooner or later, you will be needing to find your special one.

There are exceptions to this rule, but I have never met any of them. Most of us need the conventions of coupledom, family, and stability to be happy. Few of us who go through life without giving of ourselves body and soul and heart and spirit as you can only give to your own true love and the offspring you produce will know the selfish joy of selflessness.

And I think one of the real privileges of making and having a family is that, if you are lucky, you will get to have the experience of loving so much that you ache. *Ache,* by the way, is not the same word as *pain:* Pain is a horrible thing, and in our single years, many of us will have far too much experience with it, far too many episodes when our most beautiful and delicate and worthy emotions are buffeted about by worthless objects who simply leave us feeling pained. While it is popular these days to say that unrequited love is an illusion, a fanciful misinterpretation of infatuation or need, I don't think that is true: I think you can simply love the wrong person, and it can plainly hurt you lots and lots, and the miserable pain it produces, while often the result of misguided affections, is not a sign that it was not "real" love. It was just bad love.

But love that makes you ache—that is a different thing entirely. That is about feeling so connected and attached to people that you are in this life together, that what happens to them happens to you. And I do not mean this in a narcissistic or—please forgive me—codependent sense: I speak of a feeling of closeness so real and immense and important that it matters so much, it has the *right* to matter so much, and you are no longer in this life alone. I am not speaking of losing your personality, or individuality—of surrendering your own spirit—and if you were on your own long enough to really develop those aspects of yourself, that simply will not happen. I am talking about bringing your whole self into building a community, and instead of spending a lot of your precious time in pain over men or people who don't care enough, you can give yourself to loving and being loved back all the way. And if you are fortunate, if you are really able to feel the gentle, deep pull of this kind of love, sometimes you will ache with the knowledge that you have been gifted with such a sweet, tender thing.

So do not despair of the miserable example of your own childhood and choose not to have a family of your own. Do not be denied by fear. No matter how much shit was visited upon you when you were young—so much bad that it occasionally seems like the best you will ever manage to do is *hate* so much that it hurts—I still believe we all ought to take the chance, the huge and potentially devastating chance, that we will be rewarded by loving that much. As was pointed out by Albert Einstein himself, "People like us, who believe in physics, know that the distinction between past, present, and future is only a stubbornly persistent illusion." If you correct your past with good choices made in the present, then when all these different time zones smash together, they will turn into a happy future.

And one of the nice things about the transitional nature of the millennial era—and of growing up in a messy array of years leading up to this temporal apotheosis—is that it suggests a huge opportunity for invention. Clearly, the family structures that we were born into were less than ideal or they would not have resulted in a fifty percent failure rate. It is almost a political problem when so many people are plagued by a social ill that you tend to think of as the reserve of psychologists and psychiatrists, and not the scourge of public life. But it is now up to us to make and model our own family molds. It does not have to be like our parents' were. It does not have to be the way it ever was.

Beginning with the wedding itself, we can do things however we like. We do not have to wear white to the altar or hide our knowing eyes behind a veil of ignorance, however elegant. We can wear dirty white or off-white or ecru or ivory; we can wear semi-innocent colors like gray or mint green or pink peach or blushing beige; we can even wear black—though that would be trading one cliché for another, while at the same time denying yourself a rare opportunity to *not* wear black. But we can wear whatever we want, suffice it to say. We can also avoid and elope, or, for that matter, we can dispense with the whole business of marriage—it is, after all, just a legal agreement, with gifts from Tiffany as a perk—and stay in a committed relationship forever more. We can simply live together indefinitely, and let everyone else wonder when we intend to make it legal.

And once we decide whom to settle down with, we can do whatever else we want, in terms of lifestyle and all. We don't have to move into a split-level house in a middle-class suburb as soon as the first child is born; we can stay in the city, and raise kids who are urban and urbane, who think chewing gum is bovine and disgusting, who enjoy Saturday afternoons at Cubism exhibits and evenings at art-house cinemas. We don't have to give our daughters names like Ashley and Whitney, like all the parents seem to do now; we can call them Delilah and Desdemona and Jezebel for all anyone else cares. Or, for that matter, we can make completely traditional choices for Sundays at church and all things in moderation. The truth is, it just doesn't matter what we do to make our lives stable and happy and full of love. A family is whatever works.

And I must admit, in my dark hours—when in spite of my own good sense I start to think that I will never ever find my own true love in the morass and mess of existence—I would like to hope it would be okay, or even good or grand, to just kind of go it alone. But I can't talk myself into the idea in spite of all the clever feminist rhetoric and advanced philosophy of mind that I have got at my disposal. Because I just don't believe it's true. I think of the opening scene of Wim Wenders' 1988 film *Wings of Desire,* when the angel lands on earth and peers into all the different windows in Berlin buildings, and at all the solitary lives that go on in each apartment, all these people living as close together as neighbors in urban centers do, with women crying and men yelling, and everybody so all alone. Here are all these people, in such close physical proximity, each one of them desperate and in need of an angel to save his heart or her soul from this desolation, and yet none of them can know or help each other. None of them can reach through the walls to touch anyone else's loneliness, and so the angel watches all of them through the glass panes of their lives, and he is horrified by the alienation he sees.

And just like in the movie, all over the world there are people torn apart before they have even had a chance to be together, and there are people who are just dying of loneliness.

Fortunately, you are not going to be one of them.

Anything Is Possible

*

> For what are we
> Without hope in our hearts?
> BRUCE SPRINGSTEEN
> "Across the Border"

Go for it. And when it works out say, I knew it.

Acknowledgments

Thank you Zoë Glassman for everything, and thank you Jim Glassman for providing shelter from the storm. Thank you to the Brezinski-Feldman household for entrusting me, against anyone's better judgment, with your home and hot tub. Thank you, as always and most especially, to Lydia Wills, Sita White, and all at Artists Agency for years of patience and insight and hard work, well beyond the call. Thank you Stella Kane, Jeremy Beale, and all at Quartet for so much more than any author has the right to expect, and across the ocean, no less. Thank you Jon Karp, Janelle Duryea, and all at AtRandom for making me a part of this brave new experiment. Thank you Erin Hosier for friendship and assistance. Thank you Lari Markley for nail polish, wisdom, Newports, the use of your kitchen table—and for always letting me pick the movie, and always pretending to like my choice. Thank you Karyn Rachtman, wherever you are. Thank you Jennifer Baumgardner for general excellence—and a big shout to Amy Ray for keeping me honest. Thanks, Mom. Lots of love, after all, to David, Joel, Richard, Jim, Steve, Bruno, Nathan, Jimmy, Emir, Donal, Nick, Damian, Mark, Alex, Grant, Angelo, David, Rick, Cameron, Jeff, David, Mike, Chris, Daniel, Jon, Michael, David, Tim, Jim, Stephen, Chris, Rob, Jim, Brian, and Paul—ah, what might have been. God bless everyone who helped turn this project into something more substantial than I ever thought it would be. Much appreciation to readers and bookstores the world over. And thank you to everyone else, especially some people, you know who you are.

About the Author

ELIZABETH WURTZEL graduated from Harvard College, where she received the 1986 *Rolling Stone* College Journalism Award. She was music critic at *The New Yorker* and *New York*, and her articles have appeared in numerous magazines. She is the author of the bestselling *Prozac Nation: Young and Depressed in America* and *Bitch: In Praise of Difficult Women*. The movie version of *Prozac Nation*, starring Christina Ricci and Jessica Lange, will be released later this year; Wurtzel will produce the sound track. She lives in New York City.